HR DEFINED WORKBOOK

Copyright © 2019 by Cari Hawthorne

All rights reserved. This book or any portion thereof may not be reproduced or used in any manner whatsoever without the express written permission of the publisher except for the use of brief quotations in a book review.

Printed in the United States of America

HR Defined, LLC

www.hrdefined.com

Please send any corrections of this publication to info@hrdefined.com. These notes are intended to be used in conjunction with your study efforts. Property of HR Defined, LLC. Not to be distributed. Updated as of 8/2020

This workbook is not be used solely for exam preparation purposes. It is to be used in conjunction with, or as a supplement to, your other study materials.

Table Of Contents

Introduction 1

About The Test 3

Hr Certification Test Tips 6

Laws To Know: 8

Unit 1: Business Management And Strategy 18

    Strategic Planning 19

    Step 1: Strategy Formulation 21

    Step 2: Strategy Development 22

    Step 3: Strategy Implementation 25

    Step 4: Strategy Evaluation 26

    The Financials 26

    Financial Metrics 27

    Budgeting 33

    Hr's Management Functions 33

    Managing Change 35

    Role Of Hr During Change 36

    Measures Of Accounting And Audits 37

    Key Performance Indicators 38

    Balanced Scorecards 39

    Environmental Scanning 39

    Hr And Legislation 40

Steps To Law Making 41

Corporate Social Responsibility 42

Organizational Design. 43

Corporate Restructuring 45

Leadership Theories 48

Global Hr 49

Trade Agreements 53

Ethics. 53

Diversity And Inclusion 55

Organization Life Cycles 56

Business Management And Strategy – Case Study 58

Unit 2: Talent Planning And Acquisition 67

Title Vii Of The Civil Rights Act Of 1964 67

Civil Rights Act Of 1991 68

Other Laws 69

Reasonable Accommodation. 72

Affirmative Action 75

Sexual Harassment 77

Precedent-Setting Harassment Cases 77

Workforce Planning 79

Reliability And Validity 86

The Worker Adjustment And Retraining Act 89

Succession Planning 90

Talent Planning And Acquisition Case Study 91

Unit 3: Learning And Development 97
    Organizational Learning 98
    Total Quality Management 99
    Tqm Philosophies: 100
    Adult Learners (Andragogy). 101
    Adult Learning Principles: 101
    Learning Curves 103
    Kirkpatrick's Four Levels Of Evaluating Training Effectiveness. 106
    Talent Management. 107
    Performance Management 107
    Performance Appraisal 108
    Appraisal Methods 109
    Career Management 110
    Learning And Development Case Study. 112

Unit 4: Total Rewards. 116
    Fair Labor Standards Act (Flsa) 116
    Exempt Employees 117
    Nonexempt Employees 117
    Independent Contractors 117
    Compa-Ratios 124
    Base-Pay Systems 124
    Pay Variations 127
    Organization-Wide Incentive Plans 128
    Employee Retirement Income Security Act 129
    Health Maintenance 132

Acts To Know 133

Family Medical Leave Act 134

Social Security Act 137

Unemployment Insurance: 138

Workers Compensation 138

Motivation And Pay 139

Total Rewards Case Study 140

Unit 5: Employee Engagement And Labor Relations 146

Employee Relations 146

Employee Engagement 146

Employee Involvement 147

The Unions 148

The Union Organizing Process 151

Election Campaign 154

Taft-Harley Act 155

Approaches To Contract Negotiation: 160

Unprotected Strike Activities 163

Alternative Dispute Resolution 166

Grievance Process 167

Employee Discipline 168

Progressive Discipline Steps 169

Risk Management 171

Employee And Labor Relations Case Study 173

INTRODUCTION

Congratulations! You've decided to pursue certification. You've likely seen that these certifications are preferred or required in a number of job postings. They aren't going away any time soon. We know the journey you are about to embark on can be a scary one. We've been there. And because we've been there, we wanted to reassure you of two things.

1. You can do this.

2. You're in good hands.

You are reading this because you are invested in your career. Ironically, we want you to know that we are equally invested in you and your success. This journey will be challenging. It will require long hours, and sometimes, you may even wonder why you decided to pursue certification. Don't fret. You are not alone. We've built this community of resources and like-minded professionals to help along the way. And when you begin to worry if you've made the right decision, we want you to remember your *why*.

ABOUT THIS WORKBOOK

This workbook is to be used in conjunction with an exam preparation program or textbook. We've designed it to help busy professionals like you obtain certification while still prioritizing the other elements of your life. Consider it the *Cliff Notes* of what you can expect to see in your textbooks. It is often used in combination with our bootcamp or live class offerings. Here, you will find laws you should know, information about the test, and much more. We've organized the information to align with the exam format.

This workbook is not be used solely for exam preparation purposes. It is to be used in conjunction with, or as a supplement to, your other study materials.

ABOUT THE TEST

	SPHR	PHR	CP	SCP
Business Management and Strategy HR Operations and Behavioral Competencies	40%	20%	50% of your exam will come from this section; 40% of the questions will be situational, and 10%, core knowledge.	
Talent Planning and Acquisition Employment Laws HR Planning and Succession Recruitment and Selection	16%	16%	The remainder of your exam (50%) will come from these sections. It will be heavily focused on HR-specific knowledge	
Learning and Development Adult Learning Theories Training and Education Performance Management Managing Change	12%	10%			
Total Rewards	12%	15%			
Employee Engagement and Labor Relations Employee Satisfaction Labor Relations Health Safety and Security	20%	39%			

3

* PHR and SPHR candidates will have *three hours (180 minutes) to answer 175 questions,* of which 150 will be scored, 25 will be unscored, pretest/field questions. These pretest questions are used to validate future tests. You will have four question types: multiple-choice single response; multiple-choice multiple response (e.g., questions marked "select all that apply"); fill-in-the-blank; and drag-and-drop. Many of you may want to achieve a perfect score, but you only need 70 percent to pass this exam.

* CP and SCP candidates will have *four hours (240 minutes) to answer 160 questions*, of which 130 will be scored, and 30 will be unscored pretest/field questions. All of your questions will be multiple choice, and you must score 70 percent to pass this exam.

You will not be able to memorize your way through this exam. The test will target the following:

* *HR knowledge and comprehension.* These questions test your ability to recall factual material such as definitions.

* *HR application and problem solving.* These questions test your ability to apply familiar principles or generalizations to solve problems.

* *Synthesis and evaluation.* These questions combine different elements and require you to use your critical and higher-order thinking skills to solve complex HR problems.

NOTE: I'm sure you're wondering how these exams differ. There is very little difference in their content. The primary differences are how you apply the concepts and the question format. There are a lot of situational questions in the SHRM exam, so you want to ensure that you condition yourself to reading cases and not being overwhelmed by the amount of information. Many people believe that the PHR is focused on technical and operational aspects of HR. Others argue that SHRM focuses on more strategic planning aspects. There is no evidence for either of these arguments, nor is there any data that employers prefer.

The way the SHRM material is organized may seem scary. Don't be alarmed. The material is almost identical to what you would see on your PHR/SPHR exams. Both of these exams are challenging. Don't underestimate them. You are capable of success. Now let's go after those letters.

We will indicate which material is SHRM only, but for the most part, the content is very similar.

HR CERTIFICATION TEST TIPS

1. *Don't try to memorize.* You cannot remember everything. You must understand the material to be able to apply the concepts. Don't try to remember dates. Focus on concepts and apply your knowledge of those concepts

2. *Focus your studies.* Focus your studies on the areas generating most of the questions. You can tell which ones they are by the weighted sections of the exam. Be sure to spend extra time on those areas where you have the least training and experience.

3. *Study as if you were teaching.* When you get to topics that you are having difficulty understanding, break the material down as if you were teaching it. Imagine you are a HR manager and you must explain this concept to one of your generalists.

4. *Simulate the test environment.* When you are studying or taking practice exams, it's essential to make sure you simulate the test environment. It's the equivalent of muscle memory. If you've ever run a marathon without any conditioning, this will not be the time to try. You don't want to find yourself rushing through the exam because you are tired.

5. *Deliberately allocate study time.* We all know that between works, spouses, and kids, it can be hard to set aside study time for your exams. Think of the compound effect. Little efforts each day will build up to the results you want. Trying to cram before your exam does not aid in your success but will, instead, stress you out.

6. *Take practice exams.* This tip is critical to your success. Taking practice exams will help you to identify areas of development, and help you access and refine your test-taking skills.

7. *Maximize your time.* Don't overstress on questions you cannot answer right away. Be sure to grab the low hanging fruit quickly and save the extra time for items that need more of your attention.

8. *Don't skip any questions.* You have a 25 percent chance of getting the correct answer.

9. *Trust your gut.* Don't over-rotate on questions. Trust your instincts. Don't doubt yourself or your answer selection unless you can rationalize doing so.

10. *Skip the job.* The exam is made up of questions related to general HR guidelines, not how things are done at your company. Resist the urge to consider how things are done in your workplace.

LAWS TO KNOW:

This is a list of laws you can expect to see throughout your exam. Please note that the dates are not included because you will not be tested on them. You may see some of these laws overlapped in various areas of the exam.

APPLIES TO EMPLOYERS WITH 1-14 EMPLOYEES

WAGNER ACT

The Wagner Act outlined the process of forming and creating labor unions. It guarantees the right of private sector employees to organize into trade unions, engage in collective bargaining, and take collective action such as strikes. It is enforced by the National Labor Relations Board (NLRB) and is discussed in detail in the "Employee Engagement and Labor Relations" section of this workbook.

FAIR LABOR STANDARDS ACT

The Fair Labor Standards Act (FLSA) of 1938 is a US labor law that creates the right to a minimum wage, and time-and-a-half overtime pay when people work over forty hours a week. It also prohibits employment of minors in "oppressive child labor." It is enforced by the US Department of Labor's Wage and Hour Division.

PORTAL-TO-PORTAL ACT

The Portal-to-Portal Act of 1947 amended the FLSA to clarify the definition of a compensable workday. It clarified employers' responsibilities and added protections to ensure employees are paid for all time they spend working.

IMMIGRATION REFORM AND CONTROL ACT

The Immigration Reform and Control Act (IRCA) ensures employers do not employ or continue to employ aliens unauthorized to work in the United States, and that employers do not discriminate on the basis of citizenship status or national origin. It is discussed in more detail in the "Talent Planning and Acquisition" section of this workbook.

UNIFORM GUIDELINES ON EMPLOYEE SELECTION PROCEDURES

The Equal Employment Opportunity Commission (EEOC) has published Uniform Guidelines on Employee Selection Procedures (UGESP). These guidelines prohibit selection policies and practices from having an adverse impact on the employment opportunities for any race, sex, or ethnic group unless it is a business necessity (a bona fide occupational qualification—BFOQ). It requires employers to use only job-related criteria in employment decisions. It is discussed in more detail in the "Talent Planning and Acquisition" section of this workbook.

SARBANES OXLEY: SOX

The Sarbanes-Oxley Act of 2002 is a federal law that established sweeping auditing and financial regulations for public companies. Lawmakers created the legislation to help protect shareholders, employees, and the public from accounting errors and fraudulent financial practices. It is discussed in more detail in the "Total Rewards" section of this workbook.

EMPLOYEE POLYGRAPH PROTECTION ACT

The Employee Polygraph Protection Act (EPPA) prohibits most private employers from using lie detector tests, either for pre-employment screening or during the course of employment. The act strictly limits the disclosure of information obtained during a polygraph test.

FEDERAL INSURANCE CONTRIBUTION

The Federal Insurance Contributions Act (FICA) is a US federal payroll contribution directed toward employees and employers to fund Social Security and Medicare. These are federal programs that provide benefits for retirees, people with disabilities, and children of deceased workers.

TAFT-HARTLEY

The Labor Management Relations Act (LMRA) of 1947, better known as the Taft-Hartley Act, is a US federal law that restricts the activities and power of labor unions.

OCCUPATIONAL SAFETY AND HEALTH ACT

The Occupational Safety and Health Act (OSHA) of 1970 is a US labor law governing the federal law of occupational health and safety in the private sector and federal government in the United States.

FAIR CREDIT REPORTING ACT

The Fair Credit Reporting Act (FCRA) is a US federal legislation enacted to promote the accuracy, fairness, and privacy of consumer information contained in the files of consumer reporting agencies.

EQUAL PAY ACT

The Equal Pay Act (EPA) of 1963 is a US labor law amending the Fair Labor Standards Act, aimed at abolishing wage disparity based on sex.

LILLY LEDBETTER FAIR PAY ACT

The act requires employers to redouble their efforts to ensure that their pay practices are nondiscriminatory and they keep the records needed to prove the fairness of pay decisions.

CONSUMER CREDIT PROTECTION ACT

The Consumer Credit Protection Act (CCPA) of 1968 protects consumers from creditors, banks, and credit card companies. This federal act mandates disclosure requirements that must be followed by consumer lenders and auto-leasing firms. It sets a limit on the amount of wages that can be withheld from an employee's wages because of garnishments

EMPLOYEE RETIREMENT INCOME SECURITY ACT

The Employee Retirement Income Security Act (ERISA) of 1974 is a US federal tax and labor law establishing minimum standards for pension plans in private industry. It sets out rules on the federal income tax effects of transactions associated with employee benefit plans.

FOREIGN CORRUPT PRACTICES ACT

The Foreign Corrupt Practices Act (FCPA) of 1977 is a US federal law that prohibits US citizens and entities from bribing foreign government officials to benefit their business interests. It was eventually amended to allow for payment facilitation to expedite certain government actions.

UNIFORMED SERVICES EMPLOYMENT AND REEMPLOYMENT RIGHTS ACT

The Uniformed Services Employment and Reemployment Rights Act (USERRA) of 1994 was passed by the US Congress and signed into law by President Bill Clinton on October 13, 1994, to protect the civilian employment of US active and reserve military personnel called to active duty.

HEALTH INSURANCE PORTABILITY AND ACCOUNTABILITY ACT

The Health Insurance Portability and Accountability Act (HIPAA) of 1996 is a US federal law that, upon its enactment, required the creation of national standards to protect sensitive patient health information from being disclosed without the patient's consent or knowledge. It also protects participants and beneficiaries by limiting exclusions for pre-existing conditions.

APPLIES TO EMPLOYERS WITH 15-19 EMPLOYEES

TITLE VII OF THE CIVIL RIGHTS ACT

The Civil Rights Act of 1964 is a landmark US civil rights and labor law that outlaws discrimination based on race, color, religion, sex, or national origin. It prohibits unequal application of voter registration requirements, and racial segregation in schools, employment, and public accommodations. Title VII of the act prohibits workplace discrimination.

AMERICANS WITH DISABILITIES ACT

The Americans with Disabilities Act (ADA) of 1990 is a civil rights law that prohibits discrimination based on disability. Employers are required to make reasonable accommodations for disabled individuals unless doing so would cause undue financial hardship. This act is discussed in more detail in the "Talent Planning and Acquisition" section of this workbook.

PREGNANCY DISCRIMINATION ACT

The Pregnancy Discrimination Act (PDA) forbids discrimination based on pregnancy in any area of employment, including hiring, firing, pay, job assignments, promotions, layoff, training, fringe benefits such as leave and health insurance, and any other term or condition of employment.

GENETIC INFORMATION NONDISCLOSURE ACT

Under Title II of the Genetic Information Nondisclosure Act (GINA), it is illegal to discriminate against employees or applicants because of genetic information. Title II of GINA prohibits the use of genetic information in making employment decisions, restricts employers and other entities covered by Title II (employment agencies, labor organizations and joint labor-management training and apprenticeship programs, referred to as covered entities) from requesting, requiring, or purchasing genetic information and strictly limits the disclosure of genetic information.

APPLIES TO EMPLOYERS WITH 20-49 EMPLOYEES

AGE DISCRIMINATION IN EMPLOYMENT

The Age Discrimination in Employment Act (ADEA) of 1967 is a US labor law that forbids employment discrimination against anyone at least forty years of age. It also prohibits mandatory retirement ages. The bill was signed into law by President Lyndon B. Johnson.

CONSOLIDATED OMNIBUS BUDGET RECONCILIATION ACT

The Consolidated Omnibus Budget Reconciliation Act (COBRA) gives workers and their families who lose their health benefits the right to choose to continue group health benefits provided by their group health plan for limited periods of time under certain circumstances such as voluntary or involuntary job loss, reduction in the hours worked, transition between jobs, death, divorce, and other life events. Qualified individuals may be required to pay the entire premium for coverage up to 102 percent of the cost to the plan.

APPLIES TO EMPLOYERS WITH 50-99 EMPLOYEES

FAMILY MEDICAL LEAVE ACT

The Family Medical Leave Act (FMLA) entitles eligible employees of covered employers to take unpaid, job-protected leave for specified family and medical reasons with continuation of group-health insurance coverage under the same terms and conditions as if the employee had not taken leave. Eligible employees are entitled to the following:

- Twelve workweeks of leave in a twelve-month period for
  - the birth of a child and to care for the newborn child within one year of birth
  - the placement with the employee of a child for adoption or foster care and to care for the newly placed child within one year of placement
  - to care for the employee's spouse, child, or parent who has a serious health condition
  - a serious health condition that makes employees unable to perform the essential functions of their job
  - any qualifying exigency arising out of the fact that the employee's spouse, son, daughter, or parent is a covered military service member on "covered active duty" *or*
- Twenty-six workweeks of leave during a single twelve-month period to care for a covered military service member with a serious injury or illness if the eligible employee is the service member's spouse, son, daughter, parent, or next of kin (military caregiver leave)

APPLIES TO EMPLOYERS WITH 100 OR MORE EMPLOYEES

WORKER ADJUSTMENT AND RETRAINING NOTIFICATION ACT

The Worker Adjustment and Retraining Notification Act (WARNA) of 1988 is a US labor law that protects employees, their families, and communities by requiring most employers with 100 or more employees to provide a sixty-calendar-day advance notification of plant closings and mass layoffs of employees, as defined in the act.

WHAT YOU NEED TO KNOW ABOUT FEDERAL CONTRACTORS

DRUG-FREE WORKPLACE ACT

The Drug-Free Workplace Act (DFWA) of 1988 requires some federal contractors and all federal grantees to agree that they will provide drug-free workplaces as a precondition of receiving a contract or grant from a federal agency.

DAVIS BACON ACT

The Davis–Bacon Act of 1931 is a US federal law that establishes the requirement for paying the local prevailing wages on public works projects for laborers and mechanics.

COPELAND ACT

Often called the Copeland (Anti-Kickback) Act, this act makes it unlawful for employers to receive kickbacks from employees on federally funded projects.

WALSH-HEALEY PUBLIC CONTRACTS ACT

The Walsh-Healey Public Contracts Act (PCA), as amended, establishes minimum wage, maximum hours, and safety and health standards for work on contracts in excess of $15K for the manufacturing or furnishing of materials, supplies, articles, or equipment to the US federal government or the District of Columbia.

EXECUTIVE ORDER 11246

This executive order prohibits federal contractors and federally assisted construction contractors and subcontractors who make more than $10K in government business in one year from discriminating in employment decisions on the basis of race, color, religion, sex, sexual orientation, gender identity, or national origin. The order also requires government contractors to take affirmative action to ensure that equal opportunity is provided in all aspects of their employment. Additionally, Executive Order 11246 prohibits, under certain circumstances, federal contractors and subcontractors from taking adverse employment actions against applicants and employees for asking about, discussing, or sharing information concerning their pay or the pay of their coworkers.

VOCATIONAL REHABILITATION ACT

The Vocational Rehabilitation Act prohibits discrimination on the basis of disability in programs conducted by federal agencies, in programs receiving federal financial assistance, in federal employment, and in the employment practices of federal contractors.

VIETNAM ERA VETERANS READJUSTMENT ACT

The Vietnam Era Veterans' Readjustment Assistance Act (VEVRAA) prohibits federal contractors and subcontractors from discriminating in employment against protected veterans and requires employers take affirmative action to recruit, hire, promote, and retain these individuals.

UNIT 1: BUSINESS MANAGEMENT AND STRATEGY

Business management and strategy is about developing, contributing to, and supporting your organization's mission, vision, values, and strategic goals. It provides the direction that enables an organization to achieve its long-term objectives.

MANAGEMENT AND STRATEGY ROLES

There are several different roles you may play in human resources (HR). Depending on your position, those roles may include tactical and strategic duties. They could also include advisory, services and control roles.

Strategic	Tactical
Forecasting	Timesheets
Budgeting	Payroll
Due diligence	Leave processing

OTHER ROLES:

Advisory	**HR offers advice on** • diagnosis of problems • prescription of solutions • consultant/client relationship
Service	**HR directly serves** • recruiting • training • record keeping

	HR monitors and manages
Control	- legal compliance - safety - EEOC compliance - labor relations

STRATEGIC PLANNING

Strategic planning is a complete look at how to position an organization for future success by evaluating the organization's current status, where it would like to be, and how to get there, which includes integrating the goals of the primary business functions.

STRATEGIC PLANNING

- develops and maintains a competitive advantage
- ensures that stakeholders can contribute, understand, and support vision/strategy
- teaches leaders to recognize challenges, problems, and how to solve them
- encourages forward-thinking and clarifies individual responsibilities
- better allocates time and resources to increase profitability and foster a proactive rather than reactive culture

As an HR professional, you need to know that strategy can be carried out in these four steps:

1. formulation
2. development

3. implementation

4. strategy evaluation

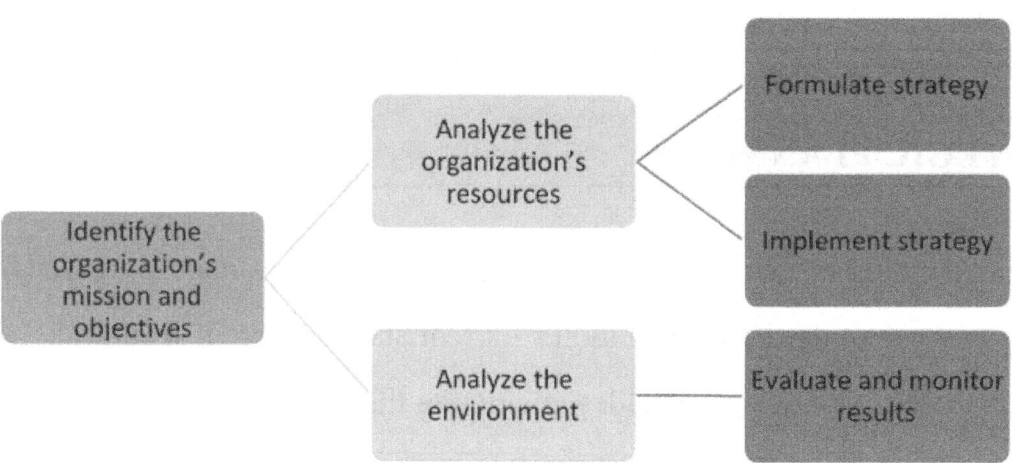

STEP 1: STRATEGY FORMULATION

MISSION

The mission statement should detail why your organization exists. For example, Google mission statement: to organization global information and make it universally accessible and useful.

VISION

Your vision statement should describe the future of the company as a successful organization. For example, Google vision statement: to provide access to global information in just one click. You should be able to visualize a vision statement. If it describes the future, what would the company look like in ten to twenty years from now?

VALUES

Values describe what is essential to an organization and often dictate employee behavior. They reflect the heart and culture of an organization (e.g., "We value a supportive, open work atmosphere that promotes teamwork and creativity.")

STEP 2: STRATEGY DEVELOPMENT

The SWOT analysis seeks to characterize internal/external forces that affect the performance of an organization.

S—Strengths

W—Weaknesses

O—Opportunities

T—Threats

Strengths and weaknesses typically relate to things internal to your organization. including the following:

* skills inventory
* staffing
* business needs
* HR resources

Strengths	Weaknesses
Characteristics of a business which give it advantages over its competitors	Characteristics of a business which make it disadvantageous relative to competitors
Opportunities	**Threats**
Elements in a company's external environment that allow it to formulate and implement strategies to increase profitability	Elements in the external environment that could endanger the integrity and profitability of the business

Opportunities and threats typically relate to things external to your organization including the following:

* Social issues (e.g., immigration)
* Economic issues (e.g., inflation, wage debates, minimum wage increases)
* Technology advances (e.g., artificial intelligence)

The strategic plan focuses on external threats/risks that are likely to have a significant impact on an organization. Less likely threats should not be addressed in the strategic plan but in the organization's risk management plan (also known as the contingency plan). These plans help in developing and using strategies to minimize an organization's exposure to liability and to respond to threats such as pandemics, terrorism, and natural disaster.

Developing long-term objectives requires identification of strategies, which are formulated on three levels:

1. *Organizational.* This level of strategy looks at competitive businesses and the markets the organization competes in. Direction may also be considered. We will consider the following: growth, stability, and retrenchment/turnaround.

    a. Growth may involve an expansion strategy, such as adding new products.

    b. Stability may include maintaining the level of operations or a prolonged growth rate either as a pause to make corrections or to serve customers where there is less potential for innovation

    c. Retrenchment/turnaround may involve reducing size or diversity of operations.

2. *Business unit.* This level of strategy looks at specific subunits. Decisions at this level focus on the best way for the organization to compete in a particular market identified in the organizational strategy.

3. *Functional.* This level *of* strategy looks at each department's business plan and translates the organization's strategic objective into function objectives to support the organizations overarching goals.

STEP 3: STRATEGY IMPLEMENTATION

* In this step, employees are motivated to manage the plan. This ensures the reasons behind the strategy are understood. This step also communicates long- and short-term goals, provides employees with tools needed to accomplish tasks, models commitment and enthusiasm, and remains sensitive to employees' emotional reactions.

* Short-term objectives are also established. These are generally achieved within six months to one year.

* Action plans to meet goals are developed. Detailed steps required to achieve short-term objectives are also outlined.

* Resources such as financial, physical, and human are allocated to work toward objectives.

* During this step, SMART goals are also outlined. These goals are specific, measurable, attainable, realistic, and timely.

STEP 4: STRATEGY EVALUATION

* During this phase, strategies are reviewed. Evaluations should be timed and part of the process.

* Performance toward objectives is measured: Are assets, profitability, or sales increased?

* Corrective action is taken: Should strategy be modified or should the desired results be allowed to take their time? Taking corrective action requires making changes to reposition an organization's plans based on changes in SWOT. Taking corrective action may require establishing new objectives, allocating resources differently, or developing new performance incentives.

HR'S ROLE IN STRATEGIC MANAGEMENT PLANNING

To understand an organization's internal environment, HR must do the following:

* be aware of the role of each function in an organization, the goals of the function, and how the various functions can support each other

* understand how the organization has structured itself for implementing strategic plans

THE FINANCIALS

One of the biggest complaints about HR professionals is that they don't understand a lot of what the business does. They give instruction without a clue about how a company makes money. This is an important criticism because HR professionals should be familiar with their organization's financial situation and understand how

HR activities are impacted by and can influence the organization's financial success. They should be able to read and understand the following financial documents:

* financial statements (formal record of an organization's financial activities)
* balance sheets
* income statements
* cash flow statements

FINANCIAL METRICS

BALANCE SHEET

This is a statement of an organization's financial position at a particular point in time. It is also known as a snapshot and includes the following items:

Assets. These items are what an organization owns. They can be tangible or intangible and do not include human capital. The balance sheet also includes investments a company has made. Tangibles include cash, inventory of finished products/materials, property, and equipment. Intangibles include copyrights, patents, software, proprietary knowledge.

Liabilities. These are what an organization owes that has been earned but not paid. Reserves should be set aside to cover potential liability, unpaid fines, legal judgments, tax debt, and accounts payable. Examples of liabilities are rent, loans, notes, wages, and benefits.

Accounts payable. These refer to money owed to suppliers/vendors (e.g., materials, utilities, and advertising).

Equity. This is what is left of a company's assets after its liabilities have been discharged

INCOME STATEMENT

Revenues, expenses, and profits are compared over a specific period of time. The income statement provides a bottom-line look at how the organization is performing. The period of time is generally one year or a quarter.

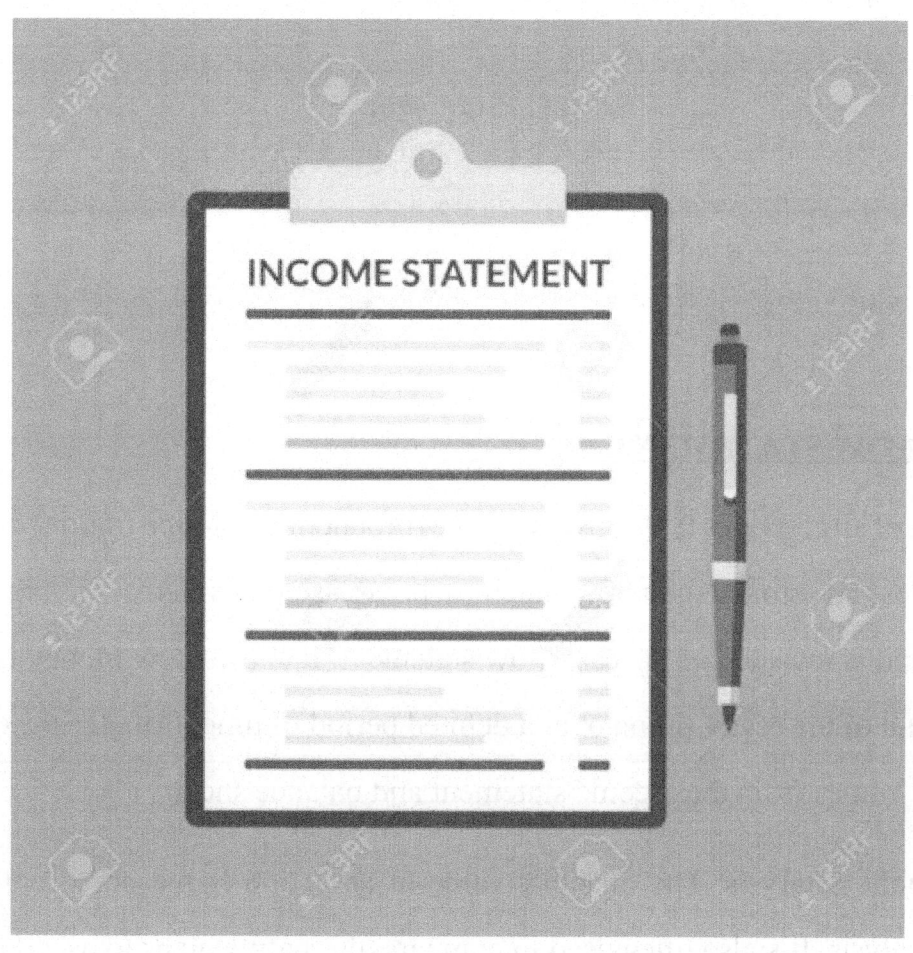

GROSS PROFIT MARGIN

A company's financial health and business model is assessed by calculating the amount of money left over from sales after deducting the cost of goods sold. The gross profit margin shows how much of each sales dollar can be expected to cover operating expenses and generate profit.

Gross Profit Margin

Gross Profit Formula = Net Revenue − Cost of Goods Sold

CASH FLOW STATEMENT

The effect of all activities that consume value (production, administration) or produce value (sales, investments) on how much cash, or cash equivalents, the organization has on hand is revealed in the cash flow statement. It shows how money is flowing into and out of the organization over a defined period of time. Data for the cash flow statement comes from the income statement and balance sheet.

Cost-Benefit Analysis: The financial value of an action Is measured with a cost-benefit analysis. It's also often used to compare alternative plans to ascertain which one has the most value. It can be used proactively or retroactively to support budget requests, defend against possible budget cuts, compete for limited resources, or provide accountability to an organization.

THE COST-BENEFIT ANALYSIS STEPS ARE AS FOLLOWS:

1. *Define objectives.* Identify the desired cost-benefit ratio.

2. *Define value and costs.* Identify all areas of potential value and costs.

3. *Analyze data.* Convert all cost factors/values into equivalent monetary units; compare scenarios, including taking no action.

4. *Report analysis findings.* Account for nonmonetary amounts/costs and recommend work based on the analysis.

EXAMPLE:

It is estimated that a new HR program will result in total savings of $10K and that the costs of the program will be $2K. The cost-benefit ratio would be calculated as follows:

$10,000

$2,000

= 5:1

RETURN ON INVESTMENT

The efficiency with which an organization uses resources available for investment is shown by the return on investment (ROI). It focuses on fewer and more tangible costs than the cost-benefit analysis, and on results. The ROI helps an organization determine if the initiative has yielded or will yield enough value to be worthwhile.

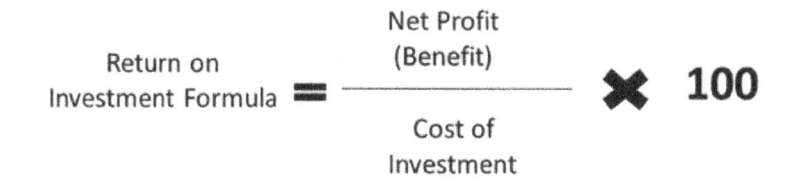

Return on Investment

$$\text{Return on Investment Formula} = \frac{\text{Net Profit (Benefit)}}{\text{Cost of Investment}} \times 100$$

BUDGETING

INCREMENTAL BUDGETING

The prior budget is the basis for funding allocation. New funds are requested based on needs and objectives.

FORMULA-BASED BUDGETING

Funding is calculated by allocating a specific percentage of the budget for each category of expense.

ZERO-BASED BUDGETING

All objectives and operations are given a priority ranking. Each unit or goal is ranked, and then available funds are given in order. All expenditures must be justified for each new period, and budgets start at zero.

HR'S MANAGEMENT FUNCTIONS

To fulfill the strategic role, HR's personnel must understand the basic business management skills necessary to perform essential management functions. These entail the following areas of management.

PLANNING

Studying the future and arranging the means for dealing with it encompasses forecasting, setting goals, and determining actions (e.g., forecasting for the future labor strategy. Are the right people in the right jobs at the right time?).

ORGANIZING

To assist in goal accomplishment, HR should design a structure that effectively relates human and other resources to tasks of the organization (e.g., If you don't have the right people in the right jobs at the right time, you must design a recruiting plan. Do you have the resources in place to handle the recruiting volume needed? Where will you find the talent?)

DIRECTING

HR's directional responsibilities include leadership motivation and employee action toward goals (e.g., talent must be sourced to fill recruiting needs; interviews must be scheduled and conducted; offers must be made).

CONTROLLING

During recruitment, HR must ensure that everything is carried out according to plan regarding measuring recruiting efforts and their effectiveness (e.g., surveys should be provided to the organization's leaders. to evaluate the effectiveness of the recruiting efforts; data points can be referred to, such as new-hire surveys, manager-satisfaction surveys, and the time taken to meet required staffing numbers).

MANAGING CHANGE

Managing change in an organization can sometimes be challenging. During change, the HR staff's role is to show personal commitment and ensure sure that people are involved in the process so they feel committed to these changes. Although, as an HR professional, you are a change agent and managing change, it's important to note that you don't have to build change management processes from scratch. There are several models already in existence for managing the change. One of the most popular ones is Kurt Lewin's three-stage change model, which shows how to accomplish and then anchor the change as the new norm. These three stages are also called unfreezing, moving, and refreezing.

During the unfreezing stage, HR must make the case for why the change is needed. Essential to its success is the involvement of all employees in the transition, which can be done by garnering employee buy-in through education. The second stage of this model involves moving from the current state of the organization to its desired state, which necessitates sharing information about the change and adapting behavior accordingly.

The last stage of Lewin's change model is refreezing the organization. This where the change introduced in the unfreezing stage is now implemented. Change management addresses the personal challenges that all the organization's people face. Here, you have an opportunity to encourage employees to let go of the past and accept the new.

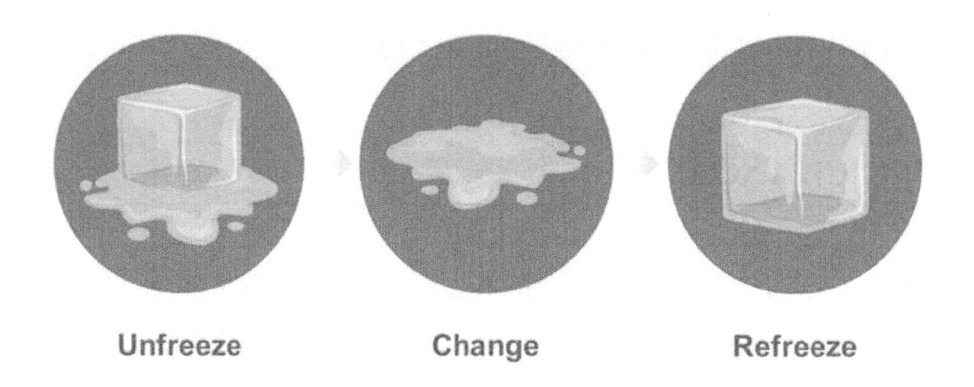

Unfreeze   Change   Refreeze

ROLE OF HR DURING CHANGE

HR can play a crucial role in helping employees adapt to change by taking the following actions:

* showing commitment to the new changes
* involving employees in the change process so they are more likely to accept and help others to adapt
* making top management and their support of the changes visible
* communicating a clear and consistent message to employees
* using peer/group influence to support change
* anticipating resistance and proactively preparing for it

MEASURES OF ACCOUNTING AND AUDITS

How do we demonstrate our value? How do we ensure that we are delivering what our clients/employees need? If you want to be seen as a strategic business partner, you must use data-backed reference points to demonstrate the return on investment.

It's important to know that the way effectiveness is measured may differ company to company. Differences aside, what you are measuring should be linked to your overall strategy. And before you go pulling out a ton of data, stop for a moment and think about your goals and priorities. Link these goals and priorities to how the HR function will help deliver the overall strategy. Consider an organization that is in the growth stage of its life cycle. During this time, additional sales personnel may be required to work on that growth. Without these sales personnel, the organization will be unable to handle rapid growth, which would ultimately affect the amount of revenue brought in. How can HR help here? By creating a recruiting strategy to attract the right talent; by formulating a compensation strategy to ensure the organization is paying competitively; and by devising a talent management strategy to ensure we can onboard and train the new sales personnel quickly. After we've mapped out these strategies, we can then measure things such as the following:

* time to hire (tied to recruiting efforts)
* quality of hire (tied to recruiting efforts)
* talent productivity (tied to talent management/training efforts)

Essentially, HR effectiveness is all about aligning HR activities with the organization's goals. HR compliance can be effectively measured by answering the following questions:

* Are our current policies and procedures up to date?
* Are employees and managers trained on the policies and procedures?
* Have we reviewed our employee handbook?
* Do we have an organized schedule to undertake and complete these reviews?

A simpler way of evaluating effectiveness is to ask leaders. You can do this through employee/manager surveys, interviewing, and focus groups that identify ways HR can offer better support. HR accounting attempts to provide information that will help managers make accurate decisions about recruiting, hiring, training, supervising, evaluating, developing, and replacing personnel.

An HR audit evaluates the effectiveness of the HR department and answers the question of how well the policies and programs sponsored by HR meet the needs of the employees and the company. Most HR audits rely on the subjective judgements and candid feedback of line managers or the professional opinions of external experts.

KEY PERFORMANCE INDICATORS

Organizations need HR metrics that measure both efficiency (time and cost) and effectiveness (ROI and profitability). Examples of key performance indicators include the following:

- absence rates
- employee productivity rates
- employee engagement index
- benefits satisfaction
- net promoter score
- internal promotion rates

BALANCED SCORECARDS

Organizations are required to balance the expectations of their stakeholders. All HR activities should be cost-benefit effective: everything should contribute to the profitability of the organization. Balancing the demands of different stakeholders requires a great deal of skill. HR managers may be forced to justify their strategies in terms of how they will affect future profits.

ENVIRONMENTAL SCANNING

Environmental scanning involves examining the economic and social forces influencing the organization, especially the long-term composition of the labor force and the future availability of employees.

Political Factors	Economic Factors	Social Factors	Technological Factors
- Taxes and the federal deficit - Social Security - Minimum wage - Paid sick leave - Domestic partner benefits - Corporate governance - Affirmative action - Attitude toward careers	- Rising health care costs - Shift to a knowledge-based economy - Emerging global economies - Increased Accountability in corporate governance - Continued demand for increasing productivity	- Age - Gender - Generational differences - Ethnicity - Unskilled labor - Nontraditional labor force - Attitude toward careers	- Advances in technology - Communication advances - Employee self-service - E-learning - Data privacy - Advances in automation - Advances in innovation - Technological skills - Process changes

HR AND LEGISLATION

The process of forming a new law begins with the bill being introduced by the US Senate or House of Representatives. The bill is then referred to a committee that determines if the bill should be considered further by a subcommittee, considered further by the entire floor of the House or Senate, or be ignored. If the bill reaches the floor of the House or Senate, the bill is debated, and a vote is taken to pass or defeat the bill. If the bill is passed in the Senate, it is passed on to the House to be considered in the same way, and vice versa. After both the House and Senate have approved a bill, it is sent to the president to be signed into law, vetoed, or returned to Congress. It may become law automatically if it is ignored for ten days while Congress is in session, or it will die automatically if it is ignored until after Congress is in session.

Why do we HR professionals care? We care because, frequently, these laws affect the way our organizations do business. Imagine if the minimum-wage law changed from $7.25 per hour to $15.00 per hour. This would affect the way we hire. We likely would not be able to hire as many people as we did previously. We would also need to look at raising the level of those minimum-wage roles. Below are the steps laid out to law making:

STEPS TO LAW MAKING

1. Referral to a committee
2. Committee action
3. Subcommittee review
4. Markup
5. Committee action to report a bill
6. Publication of a written report
7. Scheduling floor action
8. Debate
9. Voting
10. Referral to another chamber

11. Conference committee action

12. Final actions

13. Override of veto

Legislature and rules are made by agencies (for example, a law is passed to establish safe drinking water standards, and then an agency is assigned to develop the list of contaminants and safe levels through rule making).

CORPORATE SOCIAL RESPONSIBILITY

Corporate social responsibility (CSR) is the idea that corporations should be involved in programs that contribute to the well-being of their stakeholders, such as helping the poor, improving the environment, and donating to charities. We care about CSR because being involved in the community is seen as taking care of our neighbors. For example, Marc Jacobs partners with SATO, a charity dedicated to rescuing abandoned dogs in Puerto Rico and placing them in loving homes. In the aftermath of Hurricane Maria, SATO was able to rescue over one thousand homeless pups.

Netflix offers its employees fifty-two weeks of paid parental leave, which applies to both parents. Within that time, employees have the option of going back to work and then resuming their paid leave as it suits them. No matter how they choose to take their leave of absence, they receive their full salary for the entirety of its duration.

TOMS Shoes is known for its business model of providing one pair of shoes to a person in need for every pair of shoes sold. As admirable as that goal is, TOMS Shoes' fight for human rights extends well beyond it in partnering up with a number of nongovernmental organizations (NGOs) and other nonprofits to demonstrate ethical behavior, help to restore vision to visually impaired individuals, provides clean drinking water, build businesses in developing countries, and fight bullying.

ORGANIZATIONAL DESIGN

Study.com tells us that organizational design is a formal way of integrating the people, the business, and the technology. It's a simple way of asking how can we ensure we operate our business in the most effective and efficient way possible? What's important for you to know is that organizational design is more than just having fancy organization charts. The design helps us to understand how decisions are made, what the flow is, who is responsible for what, and so much more. Some of the key elements in organizational design are span of control, division of labor, and types of structure.

* *Work specialization.* Work specialization occurs when tasks are divided between teams and individuals. This is also referred to as the division of labor. Depending on the size of the organization, one or two people may do everything, or duties may be separated into different tasks. Think of how this may work in HR. Some organizations may want to hire an HR generalist, who has knowledge of a little bit of everything. Generalists can process leave, job changes, and employee relation issues. On the other hand, some organizations may have the capacity to hire specialized people to handle specific tasks. This is where you may see your benefits specialist or leave specialist. There are pros and cons to both approaches, but the key is understanding the needs of your business and creating an organizational design that can support those needs.

- *Departmentalization.* Many companies divide employees among different departments based on their specializations. Others do it based on catering to different customer groups or different steps in a process. For example, all employees responsible for payroll reports may be located in the HR department or the accounting department. You can also look at it from a product viewpoint. For example, Apple has several different products including the iPhone, MacBook, and iPod. Apple may choose to design an organization in which all employees working on the iPhone report to one structure. This design may make it easier to handle the production from beginning to end.

- *Chain of command.* This refers to who has authority over what, those they report to, and those they delegate authority to.

- *Span of control.* Span of control focuses on how many employees should report to one manager. Depending on the industry, there may be benchmarks of what's average. However, this will vary from company to company. Span of control is important because if thirty employees report to one manager, you'd have to ask yourself if those employees are getting the feedback, coaching, and development needed to be successful.

- *Centralization/decentralization.* This element of design focuses on how decisions are made. With centralization, decisions are made from the top and then cascade down. With decentralization, decision making is a more inclusive and participative activity.

- *Formalization.* This focuses on whether employees have the autonomy to get the job done with or without discretion.

- *Differentiation and integration*: The creation of an organizational structure requires an organization to respond to two basic issues: *differentiation*—how to divide the work into specialized jobs; and *integration*—how to coordinate what has been divided.

CORPORATE RESTRUCTURING

Corporate restructuring is a fancy way of saying, "We're changing some things." There are many reasons for an organization's decision to look at restructuring. It offers an opportunity to review and reconfigure operations more efficiently and effectively, and it could involve significant reorganization of assets and liabilities. An organization may decide to restructure in one of several different ways, and we're going to take a look at a few.

Re-engineering. All key processes within an organization are made as lean and efficient as possible. This idea was conceptualized by James Champy and Michael Hammer with the memorable phrase "Don't automate; obliterate." This is where we look at all the steps we are performing to identify areas of efficiency.

Workforce expansion. Growth within a company can lead to a workforce expansion. During the growth period, organizations are at risk of failing. This occurs because they don't have the resources needed to handle the rapid growth. While expansion is desirable, it, too, comes with its challenges. You have to consider learning curves, getting employees up to speed, and helping them to acclimatize to the new culture.

Workforce reduction. Another form of restructuring, it's also referred to by the terms *downsizing* and *layoffs*. Organizations may reduce the workforce to reduce costs. While this process may seem like an obvious and fast solution, companies must be sure to not land here to quickly. Oftentimes, organizations use workforce reductions as a means to solve financial issues, only to find later on that they don't have the right people in the right jobs at the right time to deliver to their customers. Strategic planning must be done here.

Mergers and acquisitions. Two existing companies form one company, or one company acquires the other. Mergers and acquisitions are uniquely challenging for HR professionals as they have the responsibility of assisting leaders with integrating the cultures of these organizations.

Depending on the size of the company, HR personnel may participate in the due-diligence process prior to a merger or an acquisition to gather pertinent information related to financials, personnel, and legal matters. Examples of notable acquisitions include Disney acquiring Pixar and Marvel, and Google acquiring Android. Notable mergers include the 1998 merger of Exxon and Mobil Corporation and Facebook and Instagram.

Divestitures. A company disposes of all or some of its assets by selling, exchanging, or closing them down. As companies grow, they may decide they focus on too many business lines, so divestiture is the way to remain profitable. An example of a notable divesture was the 2015 restructuring of GE Capital. The parent company, GE, decided it would divest its GE Capital business.

Offshoring. Some of a company's processes or services are based overseas to take advantage of lower costs.

Outsourcing. A company may cut costs by hiring an external business to perform services or make products, tasks formerly undertaken by the company's own employees.

As you can see, corporate restructuring is multifaceted. Your role as an HR professional is to ensure that you are communicating effectively with employees and acting as an agent of change to help employees through these transitions.

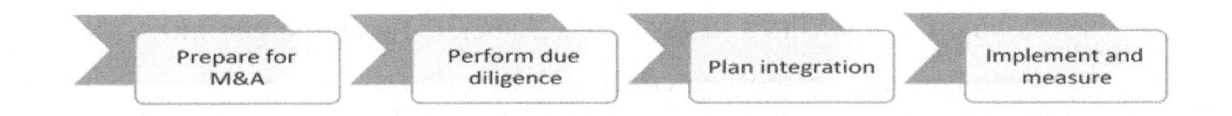

Prepare for M&A → Perform due diligence → Plan integration → Implement and measure

HR professionals need to play an active role in mergers and acquisitions right from the very beginning. In addition to the items that HR experts are expected to examine during a due diligence review—employee benefits plans, compensation programs, employment contracts, and policies—they also need to closely examine the talent and culture of the potential acquisition. Experience consistently shows that issues associated with people and culture are the primary causes of failure for most mergers and acquisitions.

After an acquisition or merger, HR should expect to play an important role in making a smooth transition. The efficiency that comes from a unified sense of direction and purpose requires combining the HR functions of the two previously separate units into one consistent policy.

* Phase 1: Prepare for merger and acquisition:
  * Issue identification, team formation and training, preparation for change
* Phase 2: Perform due diligence:
  * intensive investigation to understand associated risks: cultural, structural, technological, financial, or legal
  * compliance dimension of due diligence: benefit issues (severance, transfer

of 401(k) accounts) and nonbenefit issues (I-9, visas, FMLA, WARN)
- EEOC claim history, FLSA violations, investigations (current and pending)

✸ Phase 3: Plan integration:
- development of plans to address issues associated with merger and acquisition as well as those uncovered during due diligence
- employee communication strategies, separation or transfer process, retention programs for key employees, change management processes, new strategic plan that reflects the new organization, organizational blueprint, and staffing plan

✸ Phase 4: Implement, monitor, and measure.

LEADERSHIP THEORIES

Can you recall managers or bosses you enjoyed working for? What made them great? What made them not so great? Everyone has experienced leaders with different styles, and we're going to take a look at what some of those styles look like today. What's important to know is that there is not necessarily a right or wrong style. The specific situations determines which style may be appropriate.

Authoritarian. The authoritarian leader dictates what employees do, when they do it, which goals need to be achieved, and which tactical activities are needed to achieve them. Subordinates generally have very little input. This style can be extremely effective when critical deliverables or time-sensitive projects are involved. However, it may cause low employee engagement and morale if employees feel their opinions are not being considered.

Democratic. Democratic leaders are participative leaders. They believe in shared leadership. This type of leader empowers employees and encourages them to participate in the decision-making process. Unlike authoritarian leaders, they emphasize collaboration and welcome free-flowing ideas.

Laissez-faire. Laissez-faire leaders allow group members to operate on their own. They rarely provide any substantial guidance or direction to their employees. They believe that employees excel when they are left alone and can handle their responsibilities on their own. This leadership style is not effective when team members lack the experience or skills needed to complete a project and the guidance they need from their leader.

Transactional. Transactional leaders promote compliance through a system of rewards and punishments, which allows them to keep their followers motivated for the short term.

Transformational. Transformational leaders focus on the relationships in their team. Essentially, they lead by modeling the behavior they want to see in their team members.

GLOBAL HR

More and more companies are becoming global organizations. Because of this, HR professionals need to become more comfortable with how they manage global workforces. Some of the questions you may ask yourself before your organization goes global include how well do we know the country? What are the laws that would impact our employees? Is there an available talent pool?

GLOBAL LABOR

Some employees you may be responsible for are expatriates (people who have left their homeland and are living in another country). An example of an expatriate is Jill. a Canadian resident who left Canada to live and work in the United States. Another type of employee may be a third-country national (TCN). This is a person who is hired by a company based in one country to work in a country that is different from the one where that company is based and different from the TCN's home country. An example of a TCN is Thomas, a citizen of Romania, who is hired to work for a US-based company in Mexico City, Mexico. Another type of employee you may be responsible for managing if your company goes global is a local national, also known as a host national. These employees are hired for work in their own country by a company based in another country. An example of a local national is Godwin, a citizen of Shanghai, who is hired at Google's subsidiary in Shanghai.

The International Labor Organization (ILO), an agency of the United Nations (UN) formulates labor standards and proposes minimum standards for fundamental worker rights, including the right to organize and collective bargaining. The USA is a member

Aside from managing employees in these countries, various approaches to conducting business may be taken in these locations: ethnocentric, polycentric, regiocentric, and geocentric.

* *Ethn*ocentric. Managers follow the standards and practices of the organization's home country as the primary reference for governing and guiding international operations. As an example, managers working at Google in Shanghai, China, would use methods from Google's headquarters in California to conduct global operations.

* Polycentric. Managers follow the practices of the host country where their subsidiary is located. Taking the same example of Shanghai, instead of following the methods used by the California headquarters, managers would adopt Shanghai procedures to guide international business activities.

* Regiocentric. Very closely related to polycentric, regiocentric's critical difference is that management practices are guided by region. For example, a subsidiary in Shanghai would be guided by typical Asian Pacific management practices; a subsidiary in Dublin or Berlin would be guided by typical European management practices; and a subsidiary in California, Austin, Texas, or Chicago, Illinois, would be guided by typical North American practices.

* The geocentric approach is a transnational strategy that is adopted wherever an organization is based. These units generally have more flexibility and freedom to implement best practices based on what they feel is necessary.

Along with these approaches, we must consider the communication barriers that we may also encounter. Geert Hofstede was a social psychologist known for his work in comparative studies of culture. Throughout his research, Hofstede identified six cultural values used to explain differing reactions to problems in organizational life:

* *Power Distance.* This is the extent to which less powerful members of organizations and institutions (including the family) accept and expect unequal power distributions. An example of this would be a large power-distance society where parents teach children obedience, and a small power-distance society where parents treat children as equals.

* *Uncertainty avoidance.* This concerns the level of comfort with unstructured situations, in which informal situations are considered "novel, unknown,

surprising, and different from usual" (quoted from www.hofstede-insights.com). For example, in a strong-uncertainty environment people need definiteness, whereas in a weak-uncertainty environment, people are more comfortable with the unknown.

* *Individualism versus collectivism.* This relates to a characteristic of society, not an individual and identifies the extent to which people are integrated in social groups. So, as you may have assumed, individualism recognizes the autonomy of individuals and collectivism seeks to integrate individuals into strong, cohesive groups.

* *Masculinity versus Feminism.* This refers to the distribution of values between the genders.

* *Long term versus short term.* This refers to whether a society exhibits a pragmatic future-oriented perspective or a popular historical point of view. Short-term views foster opinions related to the past and the present. Long-term attention is directed to the future

* *Indulgence versus restrain.* This refers to the extent to which a society allows "relatively free gratification of basic and natural human desires related to enjoying life and having fun" (quoted from www.hofstede-insights.com). So, as you would expect, indulgence is seen as a value directed toward people's control of their life whereas restraint refers to culture values directed toward strict norms

TRADE AGREEMENTS

There are many reasons why a company may choose to go global including the benefits of trade agreements such as the following:

General Agreement on Tariffs and Trade (GATT). This is an international agreement setting rules for conducting international trade. The World Trade Organization was set up to support this agreement.

North America Free Trade Agreement (NAFTA). This agreement is designed to foster increased trade and investment among Mexico, Canada, and the United States.

Central American Free Trade Agreement (CAFTA). This agreement serves trade among the United States, Costa Rica, Dominican Republic, El Salvador, Guatemala, Honduras, and Nicaragua.

ETHICS

Changeboard.com tells us that "ethics in HR means helping an organization embed and uphold its values at all levels in order to maintain and increase trust. Accountability, or taking responsibility, plays a key part."

What does this mean for you, as an HR professional? It means that just as the CFO of an organization has a fiduciary duty to accurately represent the company's financials, you have a similar duty to ensure that employees are being treated fairly and equitably.

Ethics can sometimes be hard to understand. There may be situations where something isn't illegal, but it also isn't ethical. Imagine you are recruiting an accounting analyst. The hiring manager tells you that she has the perfect candidate who meets most of the criteria for the role. Just when you think your hiring manager is helping you to close out the requisition, she discloses that this perfect candidate is her sister. Now, let's be clear, this situation is not illegal, but it very well could be unethical.

Keeping ethics top of mind helps to safeguard an organization's reputation. How would you feel if you discovered that a company you were interested in working for was known for unethical hiring practices? Would this be a company you'd want to work for?

Ethics can extend to personal and professional conduct. As we continue to live in a digital age, employee conduct is increasingly being captured on camera. In light of this, many companies encourage employees to steer away from behaviors that could be harmful or possibly viewed unfavorably.

The recruiting example mentioned above could be seen as an example of nepotism. If the hiring manager is given the green light to hire her sister, do you believe she will evaluate her sister's performance without bias? Will the hiring manager recommend disciplinary action or bonuses for her sister without bias? The ethics of the hiring manager could be called into question.

Imagine you are working for a consulting company. You don't like the way the company is overquoting some of its customers, so you get the idea of starting your own business. Nothing illegal here, right? A prospective client is not happy about the prices your employer is quoting, and you recommend your own business for a lower price. This is an example of conflict of interest: your loyalty is split between self-interest and your employer's interests.

Publicly sharing inside information (proprietary or confidential information) is another form of unethical behavior.

Although unethical behavior may not be as obvious as illegal activities, we still have a duty to ensure we are upholding our ethical duty and acting as compliance officers.

DIVERSITY AND INCLUSION

Today diversity and inclusion (D&I) is a much-discussed topic. But what exactly is diversity and inclusion? Diversity programs have been suggested to improve the representation of groups that are under-represented in an organization. It's important to think beyond the definition of diversity and inclusiveness and understand why it's important to have not only a diverse workforce but a workforce that is inclusive of people with different backgrounds. These backgrounds may include different experiences, educational history, ethnicity, and gender. And it's important to approach diversity efforts with the facts.

You may be able to use your HR information systems (HRIS) to pull data on the make-up of your workforce. The second piece of this D&I initiative is inclusiveness. You can't successfully implement D&I initiatives without giving thought to inclusiveness, which is really as simple as thinking about how we make employees feel included. You'd want to ask yourself if your organization fosters an environment that includes representation from all groups within the population. How do we integrate the differences in people to achieve a successful organization? D&I can be seen as the ingredients in a cake: eggs, milk, chocolate chips, flour, and so on. We bring all of these different ingredients together to create a successful product, and that is something that we want to share with others.

Some organizations may first approach their D&I initiative by understanding the stories the data tells them. All of our efforts in HR must be centered on data-backed reference points. The data should drive our efforts and recommendations. Many organizations may do this with targeted recruiting and recruiting at universities that serve under-represented minority groups. They also may do this by gathering data from employee resource groups that foster an environment of like-minded people.

Whatever approach your organization decides to take when it comes to D&I, it's important to note that there are benefits to addressing these initiatives head on including, for example, more engaged employees who feel more included, grow more loyal to the organization, and become more productive. D&I is no longer a buzzword; it is an initiative that requires action and commitment from everyone

ORGANIZATION LIFE CYCLES

We all go through different phases in our lives. They can extend from infancy to retirement. The same happens for organizations where the phases are often categorized as startup, growth, maturity, and decline. Demise is a fifth phase that some organizations go through. Each of them has its own needs and challenges:

Startup. The startup phase is just what it sounds like: the launch of a new enterprise. If you've ever been a small business owner, you know that during this phase, you try to find funding for your enterprise, and you may wear tons of different hats.

Also, because the organization is in its early stages, you may not be able to pay a lot to yourself or your employees. Because of this, many organizations in the start-up phase may outsource tasks as it may be more economically advantageous to do so. Also during this phase, there is very little room for the traditional hierarchy structure seen in some other organizations, and employees are known to work more closely with the leaders of the organization.

Growth. As the business or company begins to expand, it's impossible to manage everything alone. During the growth stage, you may see new hires added to the team and new managers hired. As with any organization, as the hierarchy begins to form, legacy employees may feel slighted if they don't have the same access to leaders as they did before. You may start to see engagement and morale issues. As the organization continues to grow, you may see the revenue increase, resulting in higher salaries and the ability to attract top talent. This is a critical stage as, sometimes, the rapid growth can be surprising. Organizations must ensure that they have a plan to handle the growth. Their inability to do this could cause the organization to fold.

Maturity. During the maturity stage, the organization has, generally, developed to a point where it can establish policies and procedures and set precedence. This is where the culture of the organization is defined, necessitating that it remains agile enough to bend and flex where needed. The marketplace changes rapidly and getting too settled in the "way we've done things" can have damaging effects. As an HR professional, you may have the room in this phase to hire less experienced staff and invest in their training.

Decline. A declining organization is characterized by inefficiencies and inability to change. To remain competitive, leaders may implement workforce reductions, close facilities, and take other cost-cutting measures. Also, the organization's products may be outdated. In this phase, the organization may need to reinvent itself in order to compete. There is no documented evidence that organizations in this phase can't turn things around. However, aggressive measures will be needed to ensure that the organization can reposition itself as a viable one in the marketplace.

BUSINESS MANAGEMENT AND STRATEGY – CASE STUDY

(Answers to this case study can be found in the back of this book)

We drink it with a nice dinner. We covet it after a long day. When we gather for a celebration, it always finds its way to the table. Yes, we're talking about wine. Wine is the center of happiness. It relaxes our mind and brings smiles to faces. Beyond the mental pleasure, moderate wine consumption can be good for your physical health. (See https://www.wideopeneats.com/10-health-benefits-get-drinking-daily-glass-wine/.)

Marc Merlot has a business idea for a wine concierge service under the name Wine Now. You may have seen similar services such as the food delivery service Door Dash, and the groceries delivery services Instacart. Now, Marc wants to start a wine delivery service. In addition to the delivery service, Marc will provide an education card with each delivery to educate consumers on the type of wine they are consuming, meals the wine is best paired with, and a little conversational wine history for social settings.

While this may be a good idea, Marc hasn't yet outlined a detailed plan to ensure compliance, competitive advantage, and future success. As you learned in Unit 1 of this workbook, business management and strategy are critical to the development of an organization.

Before Marc can began to outline his business strategy, he will have to consider a few things that will guide the conduct of his organization, including compliance, rights and responsibilities, and the interest of stakeholders. We often call them **(1)** _____ _____. Once he's outlined these requirement, he needs to identify strategies that will help his future leaders make good decisions. This involves determining the direction in which he wants his organization to go. This is called **(2)** _____ _____.

Here Marc is outlining his **(3)** _____, which describes what he envisions for the future of his organization. He also describes in his **(4)** _____ _____ why Wine Now exists, whom it serves, and why it should continue.

As he keeps working on his business plan, Marc knows that the role of **(5)** _____ involves the combination of goals and plans to achieve competitive advantage and the methods of implementing them. He considers the competition in the market and whether or not he has **(6)** _____ or **(7)** _____ competition. He also identifies internal and external sources of competitive advantage. The approach to strategy development is called the **(8)** _____ _____.

Marc has a good idea of where he wants to take the business, but one of the keys to its success is the people he brings on board. He realizes he needs a human capital or HR management expert/consultant to help him. Since he is still in the process of outlining his strategic plan, he needs an HR professional who has the following knowledge, skills, and abilities, also known as KSAs.

Check all that apply in the list below.

(9)

* knowledge of, or willingness to obtain knowledge of, the business
* ability to assume the role of consultant or partner in the business
* ability to build relationships across the organization
* ability to assume the role of decision maker for all things people

After identifying candidates with the KSAs checked above, Marc hires you as his consultant, and you begin to work on the business strategy. As you talk through plans for bringing people to your team, you will need to provide employees with **(10)** _____ that guide the actions of the organization toward the achievement of its objectives. Some of the common issues here include promotions and transfers, compensation, and disciplinary problems. They serve three major purposes: 1) they ensure employees are treated fairly; 2) they help managers make consistent decisions; and 3) they give them the confidence to resolve problems. In addition, you'll want to make sure you provide employees with an **(11)** _____ _____ as it provides a centralized information source explaining what employees need to know about their employment.

So, now that you've outlined how future employees should conduct themselves, you should familiarize yourself with the basics of corporate finance. This will be important to Marc as he outlines his strategy. Since he is starting a new company, **(12)** _____ _____, which bases allocation on a previous budget, wouldn't be useful. **(13)** _____ _____ allocates a specific percentage of the budget to each department. We may see this type of budgeting if Marc decided to increase spending by 3%. This probably wouldn't be Marc's best method of budgeting, either. It appears that **(14)** _____ _____ _____ may be the most beneficial as it outlines all objectives, gives them a priority ranking, and justifies each expense. In addition to identifying the right budget, you'll need a good working knowledge of the financial statements informing Marc's business. He's provided you these documents for review. Identify the correct name for each of the following documents

(15) _____ **(16)** _____ **(17)** _____

Great! You have an idea of the financial documents that inform Marc's business. The final piece of the financials is identifying how much money Wine Now will make.

You can do this by calculating the **(18)** _____ _____ _____.

Complete the following hypothetical example to ensure you understand the calculation.

FIRST YEAR DETAILS	
Gross Sales (Total #of wine sold)	$925K (People like wine!)
Less cost of goods sold	$250K
(19)	=

Marc is off to a good start, and so are you. You've read through Marc's strategy, and you want to make sure you haven't missed any steps. You think the SWOT strategic management process Marc identified previously may be the right place to start. Let's review the six steps:

	What business are we in?
	External environment
	Internal environment
	Combination of internal/ external
	Taking action (short term objectives)
	A gauge of all of the above

Recall that when using the SWOT approach, we are considering strengths, weaknesses, opportunities, and threats. And now that you're familiar with that, you want to make sure your HR activities contribute to the organization's strategy. You will need this knowledge as you go on to help with the design of the organization. Before we move to the organization structure, you need to ensure that you have proper checks and balances in your HR Department. The first thing you may consider doing is an **(20)** _____ _____. This evaluates HR's effectiveness in meeting the needs of the employees and the organization.

You can demonstrate HR's value by identifying **(21)** _____ _____ _____ such as return on investment, retention, time to hire, absenteeism, and much more. Another valuable measurement tool to present to Marc is the **(22)** _____ _____. While the financials are important to the success of the business, they give an unbalanced view of the overall performance of the organization. There are three additional perspectives that would be useful to gauge the health of Wine Now and they include the **(23)** _____ _____, which shows how Wine Now is doing in comparison to others in its industry through the lens of customers; **(24)** _____ _____, which looks at how smoothly and efficiently the business is running; and lastly, the **(25)** _____ _____ _____, which looks at Wine Now's overall corporate culture and questions whether, for example, employees are aware of the latest trends or whether employees find it easy to collaborate and work together in an efficient and effective way.

This is a lot for one person to keep up with. Although Wine Now is a new business, at some point, you may think its necessary to **(26)** _____ some of the

HR functions to experts.

In the meantime, you'll need to convince Marc why getting an **(27)** ____ ____ ___ is vital for his organization. This will help you keep up with all the information about the people working work the organization. It can also help with diversity and compensation reports in addition to HR planning.

NOTE: Organizational efficiency is all about figuring out how you can be more productive by using fewer resources, and less time and money to achieve the same goal. Organizational efficiency is time based, effort based, and measurable. The main question you must ask when you're trying to determine efficiency is "How can I maximize the desirable results, using the least amount of money and time?" Think about how this plays into your hiring strategy for Wine Now.

Now it's time to consider organization structure. **(28)** _____ is about categorizing jobs and **(29)** _____ describes how we will coordinate those categories.

For Wine Now, Marc will need your help with HR (of course), a sales team, a marketing team, and a finance team. This matrix of departmentalization would be considered **(30)** _____. Because Marc believes that every function is valuable, he emphasizes a culture that extends power and authority to supervisors and employees at lower levels to make for a **(31)** _____ climate.

Marc's employees are excited, motivated, and passionate about the opportunities at Wine Now. However, these feelings are a result of the current **(32)** _____ and are capable of being changed.

As you look further into the organization's design, you want to make sure you are targeting groups currently under-represented in the organization. These efforts help to identify all the different skills available and how they can be brought together to work best. This is referred to as **(33)** _____ ___ _____.

Speaking of differences, something to think about in the future is the possibility of managing a global workforce. You never know what can happen. Wine Now may blossom into Wine Now Worldwide. But we'll explore that possibility later.

For now, let's talk about the type of people Marc will need to lead his business. Recall that we talked about the current climate of the organization. You'll need to help Marc see the importance of having **(34)** _____ leaders: those who focus on changing the attitudes and assumptions of employees and building commitment to the organization's mission, objectives, and strategies versus **(35)** _____ leaders who only manage the transactions between the organization and its members.

The first type of leader can also help encourage ethical behavior.

While Wine Now may be fulfilling consumer satisfaction in many ways, your role as an HR professional is also to help Marc see the importance of being involved in programs that contribute to the well-being of the organization's community as a whole, such as helping the poor, improving the environment, and contributing to charities. This is called **(36)** _____ _____ _____.

HYPOTHETICALS:

1. Marianne is a Canadian resident who has left Canada to be employed in the USA by Wine Now. She would be considered an _____.

2. Theodore, a citizen of Romania, is hired to work for Marc's US-based subsidiary in Mexico City, Mexico. He would be considered a _____ _____ _____.

3. Francis, a citizen of Bangalore, is hired at Wine Now's subsidiary in Bangalore. He would be considered a _____ _____.

4. Managers who are working at Wine Now in Shanghai, China, and following the practices of Wine Now's headquarters in California to guide international operations, would be taking an _____ approach.

5. If the managers in Shanghai were using Shanghai practices to guide international business instead of following the California headquarters' practices, they would be taking a _____ approach.

Now that you have tested your practical knowledge, you are going to shift gears and put on your strategic hat. Marc has high hopes that the Wine Now will soon garner a lot of attention and become a profitable business. Because of this growth, you will eventually have to assist in building out the HR Department. Using the space below, detail how you would describe the importance of business strategy and HR's role in it.

UNIT 2: TALENT PLANNING AND ACQUISITION

TITLE VII OF THE CIVIL RIGHTS ACT OF 1964

Title VII made it illegal to discriminate based on race, color, religion, sex, or national origin. this law was passed to bring equality in hiring, transfers, promotions, compensation, access to training, and all other aspects of employment.

THE LAW AFFECTS

- employers with more than fifteen employees working for twenty or more weeks of the year
- all educational institutions, public and private
- public and private employment agencies
- labor unions with fifteen or more members

EXCEPTIONS TO THE PROVISIONS OF THE LAW INCLUDE THE FOLLOWING:

1. An employment decision may work to the disadvantage a protected class even though it appears to be neutral and fair on the surface.

2. A bona fide occupational qualification may be reasonably necessary to carry out a particular job function. For example, a Baptist church requires that applicants for the position of pastor must be Christian Baptists.

3. Seniority systems are not subject to the law.

CIVIL RIGHTS ACT OF 1991

The original Civil Rights Act was expanded in 1991 to allow plaintiffs in discrimination cases to receive compensatory or punitive damages. Although the law provides for these damages, it also sets limits on the amount to be awarded. There are also time limits for filing a charge. Plaintiffs must file a charge within 180 days from the day the discrimination occurred. The deadline is extended in states where the state or a local agency enforces a law that prohibits discrimination on the same basis.

Note: Compensatory damages seek to make a person "whole."

AGE DISCRIMINATION IN EMPLOYMENT ACT –

The Age Discrimination in Employment Act (ADEA), which was initially passed in 1967 and amended in 1991, is designed to prevent discrimination against individuals over the age of thirty-nine. This act makes it unlawful to base decisions related to an individual's employment (such as pay or benefits) on the age of the individual if that individual is at least forty years old.

ADDITIONAL PROVISIONS INCLUDE THE FOLLOWING:

- The ADEA covers employers with twenty or more employees.
- The law always allows for jury trials. Instead of awarding punitive damages, the law provides for doubling back-pay damages awarded by the jury for willful violations.
- Compensatory or punitive damages aren't allowed.
- An employer only has to prove that its practices or policy was based on reasonable factors (other than age).

OTHER LAWS

OLDER WORKERS BENEFIT PROTECTION ACT

This act amended the ADEA to authorize voluntary retirement plans.

EQUAL EMPLOYMENT OPPORTUNITY COMMISSION (EEOC)

This commission was established to investigate charges of discrimination.

PREGNANCY DISCRIMINATION ACT (PDA)

This act requires the employer to treat pregnancy like any other temporary disability and provide access to medical benefits and sick leave as for any other disability. The act also made it illegal to refuse to hire a woman because she is pregnant, and to discontinue the accrued seniority of an employee who takes a leave of absence to give birth or have an abortion.

IMMIGRATION REFORM AND CONTROL ACT (IRCA)

This act requires that employers do not employ personnel who are not authorized to work in the USA.

GENETIC INFORMATION NONDISCRIMINATION ACT (GINA)

This act is enforced by the EEOC. It prohibits discrimination in employment and health insurance based on individuals' genetic information. It also makes it unlawful to gather genetic information inadvertently (overhearing) or through services offered by the employer sich as wellness programs.

LILLY LEDBETTER FAIR PAY ACT (LEDBETTER VS. GOODYEAR)

This act creates a rolling, or open, time frame for filing wage discrimination claims. The law retains the 180-300-day time frame outlined in Title VII, but now the clock renews each time employees receive compensation that is based on an allegedly discriminatory decision by the employer. Effectively, the statute of limitations starts each time an employee receives a paycheck based on the decision. The law also expands the plaintiff field: nonemployees (family) can also be plaintiffs in lawsuits claiming unlawful compensation discrimination.

UNIFORM GUIDELINES ON EMPLOYEE SELECTION PROCEDURES (UGESP

This act covers all aspects of the selection process, including recruiting, testing, interviewing, and performance appraisals. Employers must demonstrate that an employee selection procedure that has an adverse impact/disparate impact upon minorities and women is valid in predicting or measuring performance in a job. Any selection procedure with an adverse impact on a minority will be presumed discriminatory unless the procedure has been validated.

AMERICANS WITH DISABILITIES ACT (ADA)

This act prohibits discrimination of a qualified individual because of a disability. A qualified individual is one who can perform the essential functions of the job with or without reasonable accommodation. It also prohibits discrimination against a qualified individual who has a known or perceived disability.

The following are ADA definitions of disability: impairment that substantially limits one or more major life activities, there is a record of such impairment, and the employee is regarded as having such an impairment.

Major life activities as defined by the US Department of Labor include but are not limited to: caring for oneself, performing manual tasks, seeing, hearing, eating, sleeping, walking, standing, lifting, bending, speaking, breathing, learning, reading, concentrating, thinking, communicating, and working.

The ADA also defines essential job functions, primary duties that a qualified individual must be able to perform with or without a disability: the reason the job exists is to perform a specific function that may be highly specialized and require specific expertise or ability.

AMERICANS WITH DISABILITIES AMENDMENT ACT (ADAAA)

This act expands the definition of "regarded as": employees are regarded as having a disability if they establish that they have been discriminated against because of an actual or perceived physical or mental impairment. The primary focus is on how the employee was treated rather than on what an employer believes about the nature of the person's impairment. It also shifts the burden of proof from the employee to the employer and the employer's reasonable faith effort to accommodate the employee. The act introduced a nonexhaustive list of major life activities. Most of the disabilities cited involve bad backs, neurological impairments, emotional/psychological impairments, and a variety of impairments affecting heart, vision, and hearing.

REASONABLE ACCOMMODATION

This means modifying or adjusting a job application process, a work environment, or the circumstances under which a job is usually performed to enable a qualified individual with a disability to be considered for the position and fulfill its essential functions. Providing reasonable accommodation entails the following:

* An employee asks for the accommodation.

* The employer identifies the barriers to the performance of essential functions for each individual.

* The employer identifies possible accommodations that might help overcome the obstacles.

* The employer assesses the reasonableness of the accommodations, including whether they are the employer's responsibility and whether they impose an undue hardship.

NOTE: Employers are not required to experience undue hardship to provide accommodation

DISCRIMINATION IN HIRING

When the hiring rate for a protected class is less than 80 percent of the rate for the class with the highest hiring rate, discrimination occurs: the protected class is treated differently or evaluated using different standards (e.g., entry requirements for women that are different from those for men). The rule for identifying discrimination against a protected class is known as the 80 percent rule, or four-fifths rule.

YOU SHOULD ASK THE FOLLOWING QUESTIONS WHEN ACQUIRING TALENT:

* Why am I reviewing employment regulations?
* What are the requirements of the job?
* Does the job require a bona fide occupational qualification (BFOQ)?
* What are the selection rates of each group?
* Who has the highest selection rate?

THE FOLLOWING IS AN EXAMPLE OF THE 80 PERCENT RULE:

	# of Applicants	# Hired	Percentage
MALE	200	160	80%
FEMALE	180	100	55%

In the example above, males are most represented at 80 percent. To determine if an adverse impact exists, we need to compare the under-represented to the most represented, and the result of our calculation is .55/80 = 68 percent.

As you can see from the example above, 68 percent is *less than* 80 percent, which indicates that in this example, adverse impact does exist.

These tests of under-representation are complex and important, so do not be surprised if you see on your exam a case like the one below.

A day-care service is looking to hire child-care workers for its new facilities. The essential requirement is that the applicants have prior experience working with children. The data is listed in the chart below.

	Women Applicants	Men Applicants	Women Hired	Men Hired	% of Women	% of Men
W	100	80	80	40	80%	50%
B	80	60	70	30	87%	50%
L	60	40	50	20	83%	50%

Legend: W = white; B = black; L = Latino

* Which is the highest represented group? Across the board, we see that it's women, but in this case, black women at 87 percent.

* Which is the under-represented group? Across the board, we can see that it's the men, at 50 percent.

Let's compare the highest selection rate of 87 percent with the lowest selection rate of 50% 50/87 = 57%. In this example, all the men are adversely impacted by the requirement that they must have prior experience working with children.

Note: Don't get too deep into the weeds. Just focus on the data provided and make no assumptions.

AFFIRMATIVE ACTION

Affirmative action (under the Civil Rights Act of 1964) relates to employers' efforts to increase the presence of women, minorities, covered veterans, and disabled individuals in the workplace. The purpose is to ensure the advancement of those who have been historically excluded. This provision is enforced by the Office of Federal Contract Compliance Programs (OFCCP) of the US Department of Labor. An affirmative action plan (AAP) requires employers to set goals and action plans that demonstrate their plans to advance these groups.

ADDITIONAL INFORMATION REGARDING AAPS INCLUDES THE FOLLOWING:

* Affirmative action plans mostly apply to organizations that do business with the federal government.

* They are written plans that outline the organization's programs, policies, and procedures for proactively ensuring equal opportunity in all aspects of employment.

* They are designed to provide management with a road map to correct problem areas and support recruitment and selection goals.

* Executive Order 11246 plays an important role in affirmative action. It prohibits federal contractors and federally assisted construction contractors who make over $10K in government business from discriminating in employment decisions based on race, color, religion, sex, or national origin and requires them to take affirmative action.

VIETNAM ERA VETERANS READJUSTMENT ASSISTANCE ACT (VEVRAA)

VEVRAA applies to federal contractors/subcontractors, who are required to take affirmative action in hiring and promoting veterans and disabled veterans.

REHABILITATION ACT

Discrimination based on physical or mental disabilities is prohibited. Under the Rehabilitation Act, a disability is defined as a physical or mental impairment that substantially limits one or more major life activities; the employee has a record of such impairment; and/or is perceived as having an impairment. The rehabilitation act requires reasonable accommodations for contractors.

EMPLOYEE POLYGRAPH PROTECTION ACT

Employers engaged in, or affecting, interstate commerce are, generally, prohibited from using a lie detector test for pre-employment screening or during employment. An employer cannot discharge an employee for refusing to take a lie-detector test (except intelligence or other federal contractors) and cannot refer to the results of a known polygraph.

CONSUMER CREDIT PROTECTION ACT

The amount of wages that can be garnished or withheld in any one week by an employer to satisfy creditors is limited. Generally, the limit is equal to 25 percent of disposable pay. The Consumer Credit Protection Act prohibits an employer from terminating employees because of one single debt, even if that single debt results in repeated garnishments.

FAIR CREDIT REPORTING ACT

Overseen by the Federal Trade Commission, the Fair Credit Reporting Act calls for full disclosure of consumer reports by consumer reporting agencies (CRAs) so that individuals subject to them can dispute the wrongful use of the interpretation of the information. The purpose is to protect the information and make sure it is accurate.

SEXUAL HARASSMENT

THE TWO TYPES OF SEXUAL HARASSMENT ARE

- *Quid pro quo.* This type of harassment is also known as this for that or something for something. It happens when an employee is forced to choose between giving in to a superior's sexual demands and forfeiting economic benefits such as pay increase, a promotion, or continued employment.

- Hostile environment. The sexual or other discriminatory conduct is so severe and pervasive that it interferes with an individual's performance, creates an intimidating, threatening, or humiliating work environment, or perpetuates a situation that affects an employee's well-being.

PRECEDENT-SETTING HARASSMENT CASES

Meritor Savings Bank v. Vinson. This lawsuit resulted in a court ruling that first determined sexual harassment violates Title VII of the Civil Rights Act of 1964, regardless of whether it is quid pro quo or hostile environment harassment.

Harris v Forklift Systems Inc. This lawsuit led to a court ruling that established a reasonable person standard in sexual harassment: the harassment is severe enough that a reasonable person would find it abusive.

Oracle v Sundowner Offshore Service, Inc. Same-gender harassment is actionable under Title VII. The court ruling does not specify sexual orientation but that harassment must be "because of sex" to be actionable.

Faragher v City of Boca Raton & Ellerth v Burlington Northern Industries. This case established the difference between supervisor harassment that results in tangible employment action (such as discharge, failure to promote, or demotion) and supervisor harassment that does not. When harassment results in a tangible adverse employment action, the employer is always responsible. Established employers are responsible for the discriminatory acts of their employees. If no tangible adverse employment action was taken against the employee, an employer might establish an affirmative defense to liability and damages.

VICARIOUS LIABILITY

Vicarious liability refers to a legal doctrine under which a party can be held liable for the wrongful actions of another party. Because of this doctrine, employers are legally responsible for the discriminatory acts of their employees. In addition, employees should be encouraged to take advantage of preventative and corrective opportunities.

WORKFORCE PLANNING

Workforce planning is the process an organization uses to analyze its workforce and determine steps it must take to prepare for future needs. It strategically aligns an organization's' human capital with its business direction. It involves forecasting for the future composition of the workplace, conducting a gap analysis between current staff and future staff, deciding how to close any gaps, and determining how to best meet needs.

FORECASTING

Anticipated future conditions are identified based on information about the past and present. Forecasting is useful when considering HR supply and projecting future demand. Actions may be influenced by internal factors such as age (e.g., the workforce is about to retire.) This will drastically affect the labor forecast and external factors (skill availability). The following are types of forecast:

- *Judgment forecast.* This uses information from the past and present to predict future conditions.
- *Managerial estimates.* Managers estimate what they believe they will need to be operational.
- *Delphi technique.* Information is gathered from various experts, who are kept separate while providing information.
- *Nominal group technique.* Similar to a focus group, nominal group experts with different organizational functions meet together to discuss ideas and prioritize them.

✸ *Simulations*. Real situations are represented in abstract form and are often referred to as what-if scenarios. They give the organization an opportunity to gauge what could happen if specific actions were taken.

A WORKFORCE ANALYSIS PROCESS EXAMINES THE FOLLOWING FOUR AREAS:

Supply. This analysis evaluates the talent supply in relation to anticipated demand. Here you may consider the mix of skills you have in the organization, try to anticipate future needs based on expected growth, account for metrics such as attrition and turnover, and determine some of the drivers of those metrics.

Demand. This analysis looks at what the organization needs and how it will get there. You are simply evaluating the number of employees needed to meet future needs. For example, if an increase in sales is anticipated, does the organization have enough sales representatives to handle it? Some HR professionals may choose to do this using regression analysis, and others may use judgment forecasts.

Gap. This analysis compares the supply analysis to the demand analysis to identify differences in staffing levels and KSAs needed for the future. It answers the question of what you have and what you need.

Solution. This analysis examines how an organization can get what it needs within its budget constraints including whether to build, buy, or borrow the talent. Labor market trends should be taken into consideration.

If we dig a little deeper, we'll see the following pros and cons of various approaches to talent acquisition:

- *Build*ing the talent pool. Employers may grow their talent internally. They may invest in training to get employees the skills needed to be successful in the current/future roles of the organization. This strategy usually supports a culture that emphasizes promoting from within, which has its drawbacks such as failure to breed market experience, groupthink, and static culture.

- Buying your talent pool. This strategy encompasses just what it suggests: going to the market to buy the talent you need. It brings in new, fresh talent to move the organization in its new direction, but its drawbacks include the possibility of dealing with a more expensive talent pool. There may also be a limited amount of talent in this pool, obliging employers to offer an especially attractive workplace for candidates to consider working for them.

- Borrowing your talent. Employers may work through temporary help agencies or consultants to complete the work needed. Some disadvantages of this approach could be employees not seeing the opportunity as long-term and quickly looking for a role with more longevity.

JOB ANALYSIS AND EMPLOYEE ROLE

Job analysis is a systematic study of jobs to determine the activities (tasks) and responsibilities they involve, the personal qualifications necessary for job performance, the conditions under which the work is performed, and the reporting structure. The analysis is of the job, not the person doing the job, and it concerns the three core competencies of knowledge, skills, and abilities. Essentially, you want to understand what people do at work.

THE FOLLOWING ARE JOB ANALYSIS METHODS:

* observation
* interview
* open-ended questionnaire
* highly structured questionnaire
* work diary or log

THERE ARE TWO COMPONENTS OF THE JOB ANALYSIS:

* *Job description.* The description includes title, location, organization relationships, duties and responsibilities, essential job functions, non-essential job functions, working conditions, and level of financial accountability.

* *Job specifications.* Specifications include education, experience, training, mental abilities, physical efforts and skills, judgment, and decision making. Specifications for an incumbent to be able to perform the job are spelled out and should reflect what is necessary for satisfactory performance, not what the ideal candidate should have.

Many HR professionals use the job analysis for organization design, recruiting and selection, compensation, time management, performance standards, career paths, training, a plan, and legal defense for terminations and decisions governed by the ADA. The outcome of a job analysis is a job description/job specification.

Job competencies include the core competencies (knowledge, skills, and abilities) along with other personal characteristics that work together to produce outstanding performance in a given area of responsibility. They are critical success factors for performance in a particular job or specific functional area.

HIRING PRACTICES

Employment branding. Positioning an organization as an employer of choice in the labor market creates an image that makes people want to work for and stay working for that organization. Employment branding constitutes the organization's value proposition. Consider why job seekers would want to work for Amazon or Google.

Outplacement. The outplacement firm provides support and assistance to displaced employees. It would typically be used for those employees who are removed involuntarily because of the elimination of jobs or performance problems. Outplacement services include career counseling, resume preparation, interviewing workshops, and job referral assistance.

Recruitment and yield ratios. Yield ratios can be conducted at various stages in the recruitment process as well as at the end. These ratios can determine which recruitment source, or method, or type of recruiter produces the greatest yield, and which areas may need improvement.

THE HIRING PROCESS IS OFTEN DONE IN THE FOLLOWING ORDER:

1. analyzing applicant forms
2. interviewing
3. testing and background investigation
4. contingent job offer
5. employment offer

SELECTION INTERVIEWS

Selection interviews are designed to probe areas of interest to the interviewer in order to determine how well the candidate meets the needs of the organization. Organizations tend to rely more on interviews than any other procedure in the selection process.

There are several types of interviews employers may use to gauge a candidate's experience. The following are some of the more common types of interview.

* *S*tructured. Each interview is presented with exactly the same questions in the same order.

* Patterned. The patterned interview is based on the concept that candidates' future behavior can be judged by their past performance. The patterned interview has nothing to do with job skills. It is designed to appraise only personality, motivation, and interests.

* Stress. Candidates are subjected to stress in order to gauge how well they might perform in the job, including juggling various high-priority tasks, and handling challenging clients, coworkers, or managers.

* Directive. The interviewer maintains complete control and walks the candidate through the discussion to uncover what the interviewer wants to know.

* Behavioral. Employers assess candidates based on their past behavior.

* Situational. Candidates are asked specific questions about what may happen on a job.

* Group. Multiple candidates are interviewed at the same time. The point of a group interview is to see how candidates choose to stand out from each other,

how well candidates function in a group of people they do not know, and if candidates show the necessary teamwork attributes.

- Fishbowl. Topics are discussed within a large group. Candidates sit around a table and are given topics to discuss with the other candidates while observers grade them, individually, on the quality of their contribution to the discussion.
- Panel. Interviews are conducted by a group of two or more interviewers.

These types of interview are not without bias, which includes the following types of bias:

- *Fi*rst-impression error. Snap judgments cloud the interview process (e.g., giving candidates credit for graduating from a prestigious school rather than for their knowledge, skills, and abilities).
- Negative emphasis. Subjective factors such as dress or nonverbal communication taint the interviewer's judgment. With this bias, negative information is given roughly twice the weight as favorable information.
- Halo/horn effect. Interviewers allow one strong point they value highly to overshadow all other information. The interviewer risks judging the candidate unfavorably in all areas on the basis of one trait.
- Nonverbal bias. Undue emphasis is placed on nonverbal cues, such as nails and hair, that are unrelated to job performance.
- Contrast effect. Stronger candidates who are interviewed after weaker ones may appear to be more qualified than they actually are.
- Cultural noise. Since candidates want the job, they are reluctant to discuss traits

they think the interviewer will view unfavorably. Instead, they give politically correct answers to the interviewer's questions, or respond with what they believe the interviewer wants to hear.

Hiring techniques may also include the following types of testing:

* *Cognitive ability.* Skills such as verbal, mathematical, logic, reasoning, and reading are tested (e.g., performance or work sample tests).

* *Aptitude.* The capacity to learn or acquire a new skill is tested.

* *Psychomotor.* The candidate is required to demonstrate a minimum amount of strength, physical dexterity, and coordination in a specialized area.

* *Assessment centers.* A group of candidates are evaluated at the same time in one location, using content-valid work samples. You may see this done for a managerial position. Assessment tests can take from one day to one week. There are usually multiple candidates and assessors.

RELIABILITY AND VALIDITY

When you are in the selection phase of the talent planning process, it's important to ensure that all the tools used are reliable. This includes everything from the application form, which collects biodata about a candidate, down to interview questions. The Uniform Guidelines on Employee Selection Procedures (UGESP) outlines and describes these criteria using reliability and validity.

Reliability is a scientific term that refers to the degree to which a test consistently predicts what the employer thinks it predicts. It answers the question of whether the tool is dependable and consistent in predicting the same outcomes each time the *instrument* is used. The instrument, in this case, is whatever instrument is used in the selection process. Imagine you are using a scale to determine how much you weigh. The first time you step on the scale, it shows your weight at 150 pounds. The second time you step on the scale, it shows 150 pounds. The third time you step on the same scale, it shows 150. It would be safe to assume that this scale is reliable. What happens now that we've determined this scale is reliable? We will continue to use it as a tool to gauge our weight. So, reliability refers to whether the tools we are using to select candidates produce reliable results. As a simple example of reliability, the results of the same typing test given to the same candidate on two separate occasions should be similar.

Validity refers to the *extent* that an instrument measures what it claims to measure. So, while reliability asks if the instrument is consistent and dependable, validity asks if it really measures what it claims to measure. The UGESP describes three major strategies for validating a selection process: criterion-related validity, content validity, and construct validity.

CRITERION-RELATED VALIDITY

An employer tries to assess criterion-related validity using a test or assessment. I want you to think about criterion validity as an entrance exam. Oftentimes, an employer may use an assessment before moving a candidate forward in the selection process. This is because the employer feels that how well candidates perform the test is a strong indicator of how they will do on the job. If a job applicant scores high on a pre-employment test and has high performance, we can assume that the test is a valid predictor of performance on the job. Another way to think about criterion validity involves school entrance exams. For most graduate programs, schools require a GRE or GMAT score because they believe exam scores are indicators of how well students will perform in their program.

THERE ARE TWO TYPES OF CRITERION VALIDITY:

* *Concurrent validity.* How well a new test compares to a well-established test can be measured by concurrent validity, which can also refer to the practice of concurrently testing two groups at the same time, or asking two different groups of people to take the same test. A great example of this is the validity of the Society of Human Resource Management (SHRM) and Human Resource Certification Institute (HRCI). In 2014, the SHRM decided to offer its own certification exam for HR professionals. This is a new test. It is very likely that the SHRM used some form of concurrent validity to compare its new test to the tests that had previously been administered to HR practitioners. The results of these exams are provided immediately after the exam is completed. You can usually establish validity fairly quickly using this method.

* Predictive validity. The difference between concurrent validity and predictive validity methods of measurement is time. Explorable.com tells us that predictive validity involves testing a group of subjects for a certain construct, and then comparing them with results obtained at some point in the future. This research service highlights that predictive validity is mostly used for students attending college. Most universities will use grade point average (GPA) as an indicator of performance in college. In some states, if not all, a student's GPA could grant automatic admission to a university. The assumption is that a student who has a

high GPA in high school is likely to achieve a high grade in college. To verify this approach, the GPA of students may be aggregated at the end of the first year to determine if there is a positive correlation. Notice that the difference here is time. We cannot verify that the correlation actually exists until we gather grades a year later.

CONTENT VALIDITY

Content validity measures the knowledge, skills, and abilities necessary to perform a job. For example, if you are interviewing for a recruiting role in HR, the interviewer may ask you to demonstrate how you intake role information provided by hiring managers and use it to screen candidates. For information to be content valid, it must access actual work content. It would not be beneficial to administer a forklift driving test to a recruiting candidate as forklift driving skills have no relevance to the job of recruitment. Content validity questions what the assessment has to do with the actual job.

CONSTRUCT VALIDITY

Construct validity is a nonobservable behavior constructed from different mental processes. It's often trait-based and includes constructs such as emotional intelligence and personality traits. You may see these assessments when you hire executives in your organization. It is not commonly used.

THE WORKER ADJUSTMENT AND RETRAINING ACT

The Worker Adjustment and Retraining Act (WARN), which was passed in 1988, is designed to ensure employees have an opportunity to seek other employment before their employment is terminated as part of a mass layoff or plant closing. This act requires employers with 100 or more full-time employees to notify, in writing, each employee or the union representatives, of a pending mass layoff or plant closing at least sixty days prior to the actual event. It also applies to employers with 100 or more employees who work either full- or part-time if those employees work for an aggregate total of 4,000 hours or more in an average workweek. WARN does not apply to plant closings or mass layoffs resulting from a national disaster or unforeseeable business circumstances. Nor does it apply to plant closings if there is a reasonable expectation the employer will receive funding to keep the plant open.

SUCCESSION PLANNING

Take a moment to think about a critical role in your organization. Let's assume that it's the role of the CEO. One day, after being named the lucky winner of a one-trillion-dollar lottery, the CEO collects the winnings, packs up, and leaves the organization.. Who will lead the organization forward now?

This is where succession planning comes in. Oftentimes, leaders are frantic when a critical employee resigns. Why? Because no one else is prepared to step up to the role. Succession planning is about proactively planning for the inevitable things that can happen when running a business. You need to understand what it takes to retain your top performers but also how to develop others. In order to do this, you must first do the following:

1. *Identify key positions.* Ensure you know which roles are critical to your operations.

2. *Identify top performers.* It is critical to identify top performers because they are likely in those critical roles. You need to understand what it takes to retain them, how they are motivated, and how you can keep business continuity if they choose to leave your organization. Identifying top performers is not limited to your own department. It's important to collaborate with other leaders to identify opportunities for job rotations and experience opportunities.

3. *Identify training and development plans.* If you believe that Angela may be a good fit for the role of CEO or senior executive, your plan should detail if she is ready now or if she will be ready in a year from now. If you believe she will be ready in a year from now, you need to outline what steps it will take to get her there. Does she need board training? Does she need executive leadership development? We need to identify the gaps and work on plans to address them so Angela is ready when the opportunity becomes available.

Succession planning is not a one-and-done activity. You should plan to review this plan semiannually or annually to ensure that it is still applicable and the development plans you identified in step three are still in place. Having the right people in the right jobs at the right time is a huge contributor to competitive advantage. Don't get caught off-guard by the one-trillion-dollar winning ticket.

TALENT PLANNING AND ACQUISITION CASE STUDY

(Answers to this case study can be found in the back of this book)

Workforce planning and employment involves the process of developing, implementing, and evaluating sourcing, recruitment, hiring, orientation, succession planning, retention, and organizational exit programs necessary to ensure that the workforce will meet the organization's goals and objectives.

It's time for Marc to start thinking about hiring talent for Wine Now. I'm sure you imagined that this was coming based on the prework you started during the business management and strategy phase. Before you get started with this initiative, you need to to be aware of all the elements involved in talent planning and acquisition. Marc wants you to prepare a presentation outlining all the important things he should know about hiring employees.

THERE ARE FIVE KEY AREAS:

- employment discrimination,
- HR planning,
- job analysis,
- recruitment
- selection.

This is a big project and failing to provide Marc with the information he needs can result in huge liability risks for Wine Now. With the information you've learned in preparation for your PHR/SPHR exam, you should feel comfortable putting this presentation together.

All employees are entitled to equal opportunities for employment. To ensure you do this correctly, you need to abide by the **(1)** _____ _____ _____. This is also known as **(2)** _____, and it prohibits discrimination in employment on the basis of race color, religion, sex or national origin. This act also established the **(3)** _____ _____ _____ _____ and outlined the procedures that the commission should follow to prevent unlawful employment practices. Because you know that Marc plans to hire at least fifty employees, you need to advise him that Wine Now will be required to follow the laws outlined in this act as it applies to employers with **(4)** _____ or more employees.

While you were learning about the previous act, you found that the **(5)** _____ _____ _____ _____ _____ was expanded to define more clearly which actions are discriminatory and which procedures should be followed in prosecuting them. And while both of these acts made it unlawful for employers to discriminate, discriminating on the basis of a **(6)** ____ ____ ____ _____ also known as a **(7)** _____ _____ _____ _____ is permissible when there is a business necessity.

You have a good understanding of the laws, but there's more to know about talent planning to reduce liability. The first is understanding the difference between disparate treatment and disparate impact. Treatment refers to something that is done **(8)** _____. Impact happens **(9)** _____.

We can protect ourselves from either by using the **(10)** _____ _____ to determine if either exists. Assume that Marc uses the following chart to hire. With the data below, determine if disparity exists.

(11)	# of Applicants	# Hired	Percentage
MALE	180	100	
FEMALE	200	160	

Now that you have a really good understanding of disparate treatment and impact, you should also know that employers are not allowed to hire, promote, train, compensate, discipline, lay off, or terminate on the basis of an individual's religious beliefs or observances.

If any employees or job applicants believe they have been discriminated against or make a claim to the EEOC, list some of the most important steps you can take to respond.

12. _____

13. _____

The EEOC has charged employers with ensuring they are compliant with federal laws and statutes. They have required employers to provide survey data about their workforces. The survey data requires employment data to be categorized by race/ethnicity, gender, and job category. This form is called **(14)** _____.

Marc is not planning to have government contracts, but if he were planning to, he would be required to follow to guidelines set out by the **(15)** _____ _____ _____, also referred to as Executive Order Number 4. These guidelines would require Marc to also implement **(16)** _____ _____ _____. These plans include policies, practices, and procedures that ensure all qualified applicants and employees receive an equal opportunity for recruitment, selection, and advancement.

Since we know that Marc is planning to hire at least fifty workers, he is required to follow regulations outlined by the **(17)** _____ _____ _ _____. It was enacted to protect employees who are forty years of age and older from arbitrary and age-based discrimination in hiring, promotion, training, benefits, compensation, discipline, and terminations.

Having the right people in the right place at the right time is critical to the success of your organization. Without the talent needed to push the business forward, your organization will likely face its demise very soon. This is why HR planning is critical to an organization's business strategy. Imagine if Marc Merlot were to decide to walk away from Wine Now today. Who would step in and take his place? Carefully planning for his potential exit is called **(18)** _____ _____.

After an organization's current workforce has been analyzed, the next step in developing an HR planning system is to forecast future employment needs. List some questions to ask when forecasting a labor force.

19. _____

20. _____

When you consider the long-term planning strategy, you may use the **(21)** _____. This allows you to bring the experts together to share their forecasts through a series of questionnaires and interviews.

Forecasting also includes understanding how many employees you anticipate will leave Wine Now. This allows you to better plan for the number of employees you'll need to replace and can be done through a **(22)** _____.

So, now that you understand some of strategic work needed, it's important to spend some time building out the roles at Wine Now. The **(23)** _____ _____ is the study of jobs within an organization. It consists of analyzing the activities that an employee performs; the tools, equipment, and work aids that the employee uses; and the working conditions under which the activities are performed. The details of this analysis can help your organization build out competency models and much more.

For Wine Now to be successful, there are several items you must consider:

- laws related to hiring employees
- equal opportunities
- replacing critical employees
- forecasting for the organization's future
- understanding the jobs within your organization
- recruiting the right talent to your organization

The work doesn't stop after those considerations. You may have attracted employees to your organization, but how do you keep them there?

UNIT 3: LEARNING AND DEVELOPMENT

Learning organizations are characterized by the ability to adapt to changes in the environment. Learning is accomplished by systemic organization. Change is embraced, risk is tolerated, and failures are viewed as an opportunity to learn. Learning should be tied to business objectives with the focus placed on how to learn, not just what to learn. Organizations must allow employees to take responsibility for their learning. HR personnel should ensure that learning is matched to people's learning preferences, and learning is part of everyone's job descriptions.

The five disciplines of the learning organization were developed by Peter Senge to enable companies to experience continuous growth and outshine their competitors. According to Peter Senge's study, one-third of 500 businesses disappear within fifteen years of existence, and the average life span of the largest enterprises is about forty years. The research also addressed some areas that companies should consider to ensure continued growth. In today's modern world, a business can survive for the longest time possible if it creates a successful learning organization. An exemplary company provides an environment where employees are continuously learning and expanding their knowledge to maintain a competitive advantage.

Peter Senge's five disciplines of the learning organization are as follows:

* *Systems thinking.* This discipline pertains to a conceptual framework that makes patterns more transparent and helps employees see how things interrelate and

how they can be changed.

* *Mental models.* This discipline questions the mind-sets and deeply ingrained assumptions that determine the way people think and act.
* *Personal mastery.* This discipline centers on self-awareness.
* *Team learning.* When teams start thinking together, they engage in team learning.
* *Shared vision.* What teams want to create together is a crucial concept.

HR can foster knowledge management by instilling a knowledge-sharing attitude in new employees and using training and performance management systems to encourage creativity, innovation, and knowledge transfer.

ORGANIZATIONAL LEARNING

The following types of analysis are helpful in relation for organizational learning:

* *Organizational.* This analysis reveals how well the organization is achieving its goals.
* *Task*: This analysis focuses on the skills needed by the workforce to accomplish the organization's goals.
* *Individual.* This analysis looks at the strengths and weaknesses of the current employees.

ORGANIZATIONAL DEVELOPMENT

The effectiveness of an organization and the well-being of its members through planned interventions, known as organizational development (OD), which focuses on the following:

* changing an entire system
* linking objectives to the strategic plan
* using applied behavioral science
* helping organizations diagnose and solve problems

THE GOALS OF OD ARE TO IMPROVE

* productivity (efficiency and effectiveness)
* people's satisfaction with the quality of work
* the ability of an organization to revitalize and develop itself over time
* organize processes and outputs

OD INTERVENTIONS ARE APPROPRIATE WHEN

* the organization experiences a merger or acquisition where cultures are not compatible
* the organization experiences low trust, high turnover, or elevated stress
* the organization cannot manage conflict

HR'S ROLE IN OD INTERVENTIONS IS TO

* serve as a change agent
* evaluate the intervention
* help leaders manage and settle into the change

TOTAL QUALITY MANAGEMENT

Total quality management (TQM) involves strategic integrated management systems for achieving customer satisfaction. It requires all managers and employees to participate and uses quantitative methods to continuously improve an organization's processes. The benefits include finding and eliminating problems that interfere with quality. Total quality management aims to create an environment that is conducive to creativity.

TQM PHILOSOPHIES:

* W. Edwards Deming created a fourteen-point program for managing productivity and quality. The message to managers was that if the organization made inferior products, it was the organization's fault and no one else's.

* Joseph Juran defined quality as "fitness to use," which emphasizes the reliability of the product or service. He based his approach to quality management on the trilogy of quality planning, control, and improvement.

* Philip Crosby's philosophy centered on "doing it right the first time" (DIRFT). This principle established four basic rules for how an organization should approach quality management.

* Dr. Kaoru Ishikawa introduced a variety of concepts to the field of quality management, one of the most essential being customer satisfaction: the process does not end with production but should continue after the purchase is made to ensure customer satisfaction. If the customer is unhappy with a product, it is the responsibility of the organization to identify the problem and fix it.

TQM TECHNIQUES

Six Sigma. This approach to quality control was created by Motorola. It is designed to ensure products meet desired specifications through a series of step-by-step quality control and product design procedures.

DMAIC (a Six Sigma approach). This five-stage process is designed to identify flaws by establishing a specific method for defining, measuring, analyzing, improving, and controlling quality.

ADULT LEARNERS (ANDRAGOGY)

Andragogy is the study of how adults learn. It is based on five assumptions about the differences between how adults and children learn:

1. *Self-concept.* When children become adults, they move from a dependent relationship with their teachers to self-directed learning as adults.

2. *Experience.* Over the course of their lives, people develop a reservoir of knowledge they can draw from.

3. *Readiness to learn.* Adults are motivated to learn when the knowledge benefits their social and professional roles.

4. *Orientation to learning.* As people mature, their learning focus shifts from generalized subjects to specifically problem-solving topics.

5. *Motivation to learn.* As people mature, their motivation to learn becomes increasingly self-driven.

ADULT LEARNING PRINCIPLES:

Adults focus on real-world issues with an emphasis on how learning can be applied. Adults come with goals and expectations, and they appreciate an approach to learning that allows for debate and the challenge of ideas. They also like to be seen as a resource for other people.

EFFECTIVE APPLICATION OF KNOWLEDGE

To be effective, learning must be applied. Your role as an HR professional is to ensure that adult learners apply the information they have learned to their job. You can do this by demonstrating how the training applies to future and current needs, and most importantly, by explaining the benefits they gain from this newly acquired knowledge.

MOST STUDENTS HAVE DIFFERENT LEARNING STYLES, INCLUDING THE FOLLOWING:

* *Visual.* These students learn best by seeing. They need to see body language and facial expressions.
* *Auditory.* These students learn best through hearing. They often learn from reading text out loud and using a tape recorder.
* *Kinesthetic.* These students are known as tactile learners. They learn best through a hands-on approach.

OBSTACLES TO LEARNING INCLUDE THE FOLLOWING:

* *Low tolerance for change.* Some individuals fear that change will make their jobs more challenging. HR should communicate that without growth and change, the organization and jobs may not survive,
* *Lack of trust.* Individuals who lack trust should be included in training design and HR should explain strategic objectives to them.
* *Peer pressure.* HR should find the root cause of the negative perception of learning.

LEARNING CURVES

* *Decreasing returns.* At first, the amount of learning or the skill level rises rapidly. Then, the rate of improvement slows. When the routine task is mastered, the learning stops.

* *Increasing returns.* When someone learns something completely new, the beginning of the learning curve is slow while the basics are discovered. Then performance takes off as skills and knowledge are acquired. This may occur when the learner doesn't have the necessary background or the content is complex.

* *S-shaped curve.* This is a combination of decreasing and increasing returns. An individual is learning a difficult task that requires specific insight and problem-solving skills. Learning may be slow until the learner becomes familiar with the process. Then the performance takes off, but the process may start all over again when a new challenge is presented.

* *Plateau curve.* The learning is fast at first but then flattens out, and there is no apparent progress. However, the assumption plateau is not permanent, and with additional support/encouragement, the individual may make new strides. This is common when learners are prepared for the plateau and may get discouraged if they don't receive understanding and encouragement.

BLOOM'S TAXONOMY

Bloom's taxonomy is a hierarchical model used to classify educational learning objectives into specificity and complexity levels. The models cover learning objectives in affective, cognitive, and sensory domains. Bloom's taxonomy provides an excellent structure for planning, designing, assessing, and evaluating training and learning effectiveness. The model also serves as a checklist helping you to ensure that training delivers all the necessary development for students, and provides a template by which you can assess the validity and coverage of any existing training.

BLOOM'S TAXONOMY CONSISTS OF THREE CENTRAL DOMAINS:

- cognitive (intellectual capability)
- affective (feelings, emotions, and behavior)
- psychomotor (manual and physical skills)

BLOOM ALSO HIGHLIGHTS THAT THERE ARE SIX LEVELS OF LEARNING. THE LEVELS ARE OUTLINED BELOW:

- *Knowledge.* Learners can recall specific facts (e.g., a junior mechanic can name all the parts on a car).
- *Comprehension.* Learners can translate or interpret information (e.g., a junior mechanic can explain how the car works).
- *Application.* Learners can apply the learned information to a new situation (e.g., a junior mechanic can drive the car).
- *Analysis.* Learners can break down the information and explain how it fits together (e.g., a junior mechanic can do preventative maintenance and determine what would make the car run more efficiently).
- *Synthesis.* Learners can respond to new situations and determine troubleshooting techniques and solutions (e.g., a junior mechanic can train others on how to drive the car).

* *Evaluation.* The highest level of learning is evaluation because it allows learners to make judgments (e.g., a junior mechanic can determine the most reliable and cost-effective car).

A needs analysis identifies and articulates an organization's needs. This is the first step in the instructional design process. It can be used to identify the effectiveness of efforts to achieve goals, to address gaps in performance, to identify the types of program needed, the target audience, content based on facts, and baseline information to evaluate the efficacy of, and parameters for, cost-effective programs. It's crucial to review organizational environmental scanning and SWOT analysis to ensure the instructional program is aligned with strategic goals.

Often, organizations don't conduct a needs analysis because they lack the resources and support, the analysis is time-consuming, it's difficult to summarize findings into objective data, and managers may prefer action over research. The following chart explains the characteristics of each step:

Assessment/Analysis	<ul><li>Gather data and identify needs.</li><li>Collect different types of information from various methods to validate data.</li><li>Determine needs that can be met by training interventions.</li></ul>
Design	<ul><li>Compose goals and objectives.</li><li>Define the target audience.</li><li>Select instructional designer.</li></ul>

Development	- Draw upon learning content that already exists in the organization to avoid reinventing the wheel and promote consistency.
- Determine the type of training program; skills training is most common.
- Determine the training delivery method.
Implementation	- Implement a pilot program.
- Revisit content; make adjustments based on the pilot program.
- Schedule a program.
- Select a facilitator.
Evaluation	- The effectiveness of the program is measured.

KIRKPATRICK'S FOUR LEVELS OF EVALUATING TRAINING EFFECTIVENESS

How do you analyze and evaluate the effectiveness of the training you offer to your employees? There are various models a business can adopt to gauge the success of a training program. The Kirkpatrick model is one of the top-ranked models that has proved useful in analyzing and evaluating the result of an employee training program or an educational system. The following levels show the effectiveness of the training:

1. *Reaction*. This initial level demonstrates how participants feel about the training.

2. *Learning*. This second level demonstrates how participants have increased or otherwise changed their knowledge skills and abilities.

3. *Behavior.* The third level demonstrates how participants have changed their behavior on the job.

4. *Results.* The fourth level demonstrates how the program has affected the organization's goals.

TALENT MANAGEMENT

Managing talent involves the development and integration of HR processes that attract, engage, and retain the KSAs of employees to meet current and future business needs. The goal is to increase workplace productivity. As a strategic approach to managing human capital, it should be aligned with strategic goals, executed as a continual process, ever-evolving and changing with the business direction of the organization.

Managing talent also involves retention (ability to keep talented employees).

PERFORMANCE MANAGEMENT

The process of maintaining or improving employee job performance through the use of performance assessment tools, coaching, counseling, and providing continuous feedback is known as performance management. Development plans and individuals' actions contribute to organizational goals and the professional growth of an employee.

Performance management is also about values: what is important and how business is done. This includes putting the customer first, treating employees in the same way as customers are treated, conducting business fairly and honestly, demonstrating creativity and innovation, and using teamwork to achieve goals. Values are displayed through behavior.

In setting performance standards, HR should consider behaviors and results. Employee performance standards must be communicated to the organization as a whole and must be clearly defined so employees understand the expected behavior. For an individual to meet job expectations, there should be a direct relationship between the employee job description, job competencies required, and performance plan goals and objectives.

PERFORMANCE APPRAISAL

The purpose of a performance appraisal is to

* provide the employee with useful feedback and counseling
* use the appraisal to allocate rewards and opportunities
* help to determine employees' aspirations and planning development needs

Performance appraisal can improve productivity through feedback, identification of training and development needs, communication of expectations, and fostering commitment and mutual understanding. Appraisals should be conducted continuously for individuals and for groups:

* *Individual appraisals.* Employees are observed on the job. Their strengths and weaknesses are observed. They are rated on the progress of previously stated goals, and they are given reinforcing and corrective feedback, with goals set for performance improvement.

* *Group appraisals.* Standards must be applied evenly across a group during the appraisal.

APPRAISAL METHODS

* *Category rating.* This method is the least sophisticated means of appraising performance. It requires the appraiser to mark an employee's level of performance on a designated form.

* *Graphic scale.* This method is the most common. The appraiser checks the most appropriate place on the scale for each task listed.

* *Forced choice.* This is a variation of the checklist method in which the appraiser is required to check two of four statements, one statement that best describes the employee and one that least describes the employee. Constructing valid explanations is difficult.

* *Comparative.* This method directly compare the performance of each employee with that of the others.

* *Ranking.* This method ranks employees from best to poorest. The appraiser's bias and varying performance standards may limit the effectiveness of this method.

* *Paired comparison.* This method pairs each employee with every other employee, one at a time, using the same scale. The paired comparison method requires a lot of time.

* *Forced distribution rates.* Employees are rated by placing them at different points along a bell-shaped curve, usually divided into five sections. Managers are challenged to explain positions on the curve.

- *Narrative.* This method requires appraisers to submit written narrative performance reports.

- *Essay.* This method involves responding in writing to specific topics, which requires the appraiser to have good writing ability. It is time-consuming and difficult to quantify.

- *Critical incidents.* This method requires recording positive and negative actions for the entire rating period, which can be time-consuming

- *Field review.* This method requires HR to meet with supervisors to gather information and compile data for analysis. It gives HR significant control, but it may be time-consuming

- *Management by objectives (MBO).* Set goals are used to rate employee performance. This method fosters communication and requires a strategic plan. Employees are encouraged to attain a higher level of commitment and performance because, with this method, objectives are clearly defined and measurable.

- *Behaviorally anchored rating scale (BARS).* Examples of desirable and undesirable behavior are described. Patterns are then measured against a range of performance levels.

CAREER MANAGEMENT

We've spent a lot of time considering how we attract employees, with a focus on competitive advantage, outstanding benefits, and other important incentives. But it's also important to spend an adequate amount of time focusing on employee retention, which is where career management comes in. It is a shared responsibility between employers and employees and a process that helps employees take control of their careers and identify new opportunities. It's also referred to as career pathing: HR identifies where employees are today and where they want to be. The space in between is what will help build out that plan.

A variety of learning-related can be offered to facilitate career management including the following:

Training programs. They may be for technical skills or soft skills. They may be job specific or more general. Different HR roles call for different skills. HR professionals interested in employee relations, may want to focus on technical training related to investigations and scoping. HR professionals interested in becoming an HR business partner may concentrate their skills training on influence development.

Coaching/shadowing. Throughout the life cycle of an employee, there may be times when training is not applicable. However, we may spend time coaching employees on how to handle various situations or allow them to shadow someone handling a particular scenario.

It's important to remember that career management may not always mean a promotion or an increase in pay. Many people are experience deficient, so any time they get a chance to gain new experiences, they are still winning.

In a nutshell, it's important to spend equal amounts of time developing tangible action plans to invest in high-potential employees. All the attraction tactics will have been for nothing if we don't give attention to retention as well.

LEARNING AND DEVELOPMENT CASE STUDY

(Answers to this case study can be found in the back of this book.)

Wine Now is growing rapidly. During this phase of the organizational lifecycle, Marc knows that he must not only have people who can handle the growth but also trained employees. He's become aware that to ensure the success of his business, he must outline training for his employees. He understands that through training, employees are able to acquire new knowledge, new skills, and behavior. Based on the profiles of his current workforce, he believes most of his employees have **(1)** _____, which is more general in nature. However, he knows that as he plans to move his company forward, he will need to provide **(2)** _____, which will equip his employees with specific skills and knowledge.

Marc has a lot to think about. He wants to be sure that he taps into the **(3)** _____ knowledge that refers to knowledge based on individual experience. This can be key to developing best practices. On the other hand, he knows that he must consider something more formal. This type of knowledge is generally found in manuals and is often referred to as **(4)** _____.

When you wrapped up your presentation on talent planning, a looming question remained: now that we have the employees, how do we keep them?

Your retention strategy must start once a candidate accepts the job offer because it significantly shapes that employee's experience at your organization. As you outline the training needed, **(5)** _____ _____

_____ should be at the top of your list. This program provides employees with information regarding what they need to know immediately and generally occurs over one to two days. It could include working hours, cafeteria hours, first aid supplies, and whom to contact in case of emergencies. Keen attention to, and support of, this program can have a positive impact on the expectations and satisfaction of your new employees.

One of the ways the aforementioned program differs from **(6)** _____ is in terms of length. Whereas the previously mentioned program occurs over one to two days, this program can last from three to eighteen months, allowing you to properly integrate employees into the new environment. To show them the ropes, you can match them with mentors, who may assist in navigating unfamiliar areas and also regularly check the progress of your new hires.

While these two programs have been proven helpful in retaining employees, the learning doesn't stop there. In order to maintain a competitive advantage, you would want Wine Now to be seen as a learning organization. These organizations are always equipping themselves and their employees with the tools needed to stay ahead in the market. However, doing this can be expensive and timely. You want to ensure that you are investing time and resources in the right places.

It's exciting, I know. But before you run off to develop a training program, it's important to stop and consider how these programs should be developed and implemented. We can do this by using the **(7)** ___ ___ ___ ___ ___ model. Use the space below to outline each step in this process and a few actionable items associated with each:

Training employees and watching them develop can have a positive impact on your bottom line. It's imperative that you not only train your employees but also have ways of measuring if what they learned has been retained and applied. You can first do this by understanding learning styles. List the three learning styles below:

8. _____

9. _____

10. _____

Most training programs are based on the organization's preferred learning style. They may be designed to change behavior, increase productivity, or enhance internal business processes. You will be able to evaluate how effective your training program is by evaluating these four items:

11. _____

12. _____

13. _____

14. _____

There is so much to consider when training and developing employees. You have to ensure you have the right people in the right jobs with the right skills at all times. But now that you've hired them and trained them, what else is left to do?

UNIT 4: TOTAL REWARDS

All compensation and benefits systems need to support their organization's missions and strategies. Generally, organizations have a strategic business plan that should be updated periodically.

Total rewards refers to all forms of financial and nonfinancial returns that employees receive from their employers including

- direct compensation
- pay systems
- indirect compensation
- benefits and recognition programs

FAIR LABOR STANDARDS ACT (FLSA)

This act was designed to protect workers and address conditions that burdened the American economy during the Great Depression.

- It addresses organizations whose employees engage in interstate commerce, produce goods for interstate commerce, or handle/sell/work on products that were produced for interstate commerce.
- It applies to employers with over $500K in annual business, and public sector (hospitals, schools, government agencies, etc.)

* Independent contractors/self-employed are not covered.

How the FLSA Affects Compensation

EXEMPT EMPLOYEES

Exempt employees are excluded from minimum wage and overtime requirements. They must work in a bona fide manner (executive, administrative, professional, or outside sales position). They must meet specific tests regarding their duties and cannot be paid less than $455/week, or $23,660/year.

NONEXEMPT EMPLOYEES

Nonexempt employees are not excluded from minimum wage pay requirements and are entitled to overtime.

INDEPENDENT CONTRACTORS

Independent contractors set their hours, work off-site, and on specific projects. They set their rate, and are paid by the job rather than by the hour. They have the opportunity for profit and loss and furnish their own tools and training.

FLSA Special Exemption Considerations	
Executive exemption	This exemption applies to those with primary responsibility for the management of an organization, subdivision, or department. They direct the work of at least two employees, have authority to hire/fire other employees, and affect promotion decisions.
Administrative exemption	the work includes the exercise of discretion and independent judgment concerning matters of significance.
Professional exemption	The work requires advanced knowledge and is defined as predominantly intellectual in character, requiring the regular exercise of discretion and judgment. It be in the field of science or learning and is customarily acquired by a prolonged course of specialized intellectual instruction (e.g., doctors, lawyers, teachers, engineers, pharmacists).
Creative professional exemption	The work primarily requires invention, imagination, originality, or talent in a recognized field of artistic or creative endeavor (e.g., music, writing, acting, graphic arts).
Highly compensated employees	These professionals are exempt from the wage and hour law. They are office or nonmanual workers who earn $100K or more annually and regularly perform at least one of the duties of an exempt category.

Outside sales exemption	These workers are regularly engaged away from the employer's place of business. They are not subject to minimum-wage regulations and may not draw a fixed-base salary if they make commissions.
Computer exemption	This applies to computer systems analysts, computer programmers, software engineers, or similarly skilled computer workers whose primary duties consist of application, design, development of software documentation, and the creation or modification of computer programs.

Job descriptions become an essential document for determining FLSA status. It's important to remember that FLSA status is determined by the job, not the person.

TYPES OF COMPENSATION

OVERTIME

Overtime is paid at 1.5 times the regular rate for more than forty hours worked in any workweek. Whether overtime should or should not be paid is determined by the specific situation:

* *Unworked time.* No overtime is paid for unworked time such as sick leave, holidays, vacations, jury duty, or similar.

* *Employer restrictions.* An employer is subject to pay overtime if the employer restricts the employee's activities and does not allow for personal movement.

* *Waiting time.* If an employee arrives early for an assignment, the employer does not have to pay the employee for waiting. However, if the employee

checks emails and helps out other workers while waiting for the assignment to begin, this becomes compensable time. Also, the clock starts as soon as the shift begins, even if there is no work, so this waiting time is compensable. If a machine breaks down and the employee has to wait for it to be fixed, the waiting time is also compensable.

TRAVEL TIME

- Determining whether travel time should be paid depends on the specific situation.
- The Employee Commuting Flexibility Act clarifies that commuting time is not paid work time, even when the employee uses a paid work vehicle.
- However, nonexempt employees who drive service vehicles to perform work on their way home or respond to emergency calls after work should be paid travel pay (in addition to overtime pay).
- Employees who travel during the day from one location to another should be paid for travel time and this includes traveling to meetings.

TRAINING

Training is generally paid unless 1) voluntary, 2) attendance is outside the employee's regular work hours, 3) the event is not directly job related, and 4) the employee performs no product work during this period (all four conditions must be met).

COMPARABLE WORTH

This theory looks at different jobs that women and men hold with comparable skills, effort, responsibility, and working conditions. Some exceptions to equal pay include

* seniority systems
* merit systems
* the difference in quality or quantity of work
* geographic work differentials or any factor other than gender.

EXTERNAL AND INTERNAL EQUITY

External equity involves comparing an organization's compensation levels and practices to those of other organizations that are in the same market and competing for the same employees (while maintaining a positive bottom line).

Internal equity correlates what employees bring to the market with how the organization rewards them and is designed to compensate employers appropriately.

Employers must decide which strategy to take.

* If they want to match the market, they may be more aligned with their competitors.
* If they want to lead the market, they may be considered the highest payer.
* If they choose to lag behind the market, they may be considered one of the lowest payers.

COMPENSATION BASED ON JOB EVALUATION

Job evaluation is concerned with the value of the job. We determine relative worth by establishing a hierarchy of jobs. It's typically done after the job analysis and focuses on the job description and specifications. Job evaluation can use nonquantitative and quantitative methods. The following are nonquantitative methods:

Nonquantitative. This method (whole job method) tries to establish a relative order of jobs by evaluating the entire job and placing jobs in a hierarchical order without a numeric value assigned to each job. As a result, the value an organization places on one job over another is obvious, but how much more it is valued is not.

Job Ranking. This method involves establishing a hierarchy of jobs from lowest to highest based on each job's overall value to the organization. The ranking method evaluates the whole job, rather than parts of it and compares one job to another. It is easy to explain and inexpensive, but it may not be clear why one job is valued over another. There may not be much of a difference between jobs, making the ranking ineffective. It's also not feasible when evaluating a large number of positions.

Paired comparison. If there are many jobs to evaluate, this method may be used to compare each job with every other job being assessed. The job with the largest number of greater-than rankings is the highest-ranked job, and so on. A matrix is used to compare all possible pairs of jobs.

Job classification. This method involves grouping jobs into a predetermined number of grades or classifications, each having a class description to use for job comparisons.

Quantitative methods attempt to establish how much more one job is worth than another job by using a scaling system:

Point-factor. This method involves using specific compensable factors to evaluate relative job worth. It is less complex and commonly used.

Compensable factors. This method is used to determine which jobs are worth more than others. It reflects how the organization perceives the job adds value to the organization. Job descriptions should document the compensable factors and we may see these used in the Hay method.

Factor comparison. This method is more complex than ranking, classifications, or the point-factor method and rarely used. It involves ranking each job by each selected compensable factor and then identifying dollar values for each level of each factor to develop a pay rate.

PAY SURVEYS

Pay surveys are used to collect info on prevailing market rates and often include topics such as starting wage rates, base pay, pay ranges, out pay, shift differential, and incentive plans. Many employers may use private or public surveys.

PAY GRADES

Pay grades are used to group jobs that have approximately the same relative or external worth. All jobs within a particular grade are paid the same rate within the same pay range. There are no fixed rules on the number of pay grades. Pay grades allows the compensation team to avoid determining a separate pay range for each job.

PAY RANGES

Ranges set the upper and lower bounds of possible compensation for individuals whose jobs fall in a pay grade. Pay ranges are created for each grade. The market data from surveys is used to develop the midpoint, and then the organization determines minimums and maximums. There should be an overlap between pay ranges to make it possible for more experienced people to be paid more and for promotional opportunities that don't correspond to large salary increases.

COMPA-RATIOS

Compa-ratio compares an employee's pay with the midpoint of the pay grade/range, based on a numerical representation of the wage level, and it indicates how the employee's pay compares to that of others doing the same job.

BROADBANDING

This method combines several salary grades or job classifications with narrow pay ranges into one band with a wider range spread and is used when an organization has too many pay grades with narrow midpoints.

PAYROLL

The responsibilities of payroll staff include the following:

* compliance with federal, state, and local laws
* periodic reporting
* record retention
* control and security

BASE-PAY SYSTEMS

* Base pay (hourly or salary) is structured by:
* *Single-or-flat rate.* In this system, each incumbent of a job has the same pay regardless of performance or seniority and the rate corresponds with target

market data. It works well for routine, easy-to-administer jobs, but does not reflect individual performance, seniority, or skill differences.

* *Time-base/step-based.* In this system, employees' pay rate is based on the longevity of the job. Pay increases occur following a predetermined schedule of steps. People hired or promoted usually start at the first step. The system rewards longevity and is best suited to jobs where skills are learned over time. This does not generally reflect performance differences.

* *Automatic step-rate.* This system divides pay into four to seven ranges, which are 3 to 7 percent apart. At prescribed intervals, employees with the required seniority receive a one-step increase. This system is most common in unions or the public sector.

* *Step-rate with variability.* This system is similar to the automatic step-rate system in using performance considerations, but size or timing may vary if performance is above or below standard.

* *Performance-based/merit-based.* In this system, an individual's performance is the basis for the amount and timing of pay increases. Employees are hired on or near the pay range minimum. With this system, an employer must be able to clearly defend differences in salary increases as well as the performance appraisal methods used to determine differences.

* *Productivity-based.* This system is based on employees' output. It is used for assembly line work when units of output can be measured, a clear relationship exists between employee effort and output, the job is standardized, quality is less important than quantity, and costs are known and precise. It may result in workforce inflexibility.

Red circle rate	These rates are above the range maximum. They can occur when long-term employees reach the top of the bracket and aren't promoted or when someone has been bumped down to a lower-level job. Sometimes the rate is frozen, or, alternatively, the employee receives a lump sum award equal to a pay increase. If it happens often, it might indicate that the organization is a lagger and needs to adjust pay ranges.
Green circle rate	The rate is below the minimum range. This can happen when an organization promotes an employee or "tries out" an employee. Generally, employees should be given pay raises as soon as they meet the minimum requirements for the job.
Pay/wage compression	Compression occurs when there is only a small difference in pay among employees, regardless of their experience, skills, level, or seniority. It can be caused by escalation in competitive hiring rates when there is not enough difference between pay levels or when unionized rates overtake supervisory or nonunion rates.
Cost-of-living adjustment	Periodic compensation payment based on the Consumer Price Index (CPI) is given to eligible employees.
General pay increase	All employees (or a class of employees) receive a pay increase based on local competitive market requirements. It is awarded regardless of employee performance.
Lump sum increase or performance bonus	This is a one-time payment by a red circle employer.

Market-based increase/equity increase	They are used to keep a competitive advantage in attracting or retaining current employees.
Differential pay	This type of pay depends upon logistics surrounding the execution of job duties and is not added to the employee's base pay. It could vary based on the time/day of the shift.
Incentive pay	This is awarded for performance beyond normal expectations and is designed to motivate employees to perform at higher levels.
Line of sight	Employees must be able to see how their performance directly impacts their pay for incentive pay plans to be effective.
Golden handcuffs	This approach makes it difficult for an employee to leave the organization without causing a significant loss in pay.

PAY VARIATIONS

GROUP INCENTIVE PLANS

These plans are used when it is difficult to measure individual performance or when cooperation is needed to complete a task:

* *Gainsharing plans.* A portion of the gains is shared with a group and each group member receives the same cash award (e.g., Scanlon Plan).

* *Group performance incentives.* Group members are rewarded for meeting or exceeding performance standards. Each member receives the same pay, and performance standards are predetermined

ORGANIZATION-WIDE INCENTIVE PLANS

PROFIT SHARING

Profit-sharing plans allow employees to "partner" with management and reap the direct benefits of profitability.

* *Cash profit-sharing.* Employees share in the organization's profitability.

* *Deferred profit-sharing.* A percentage of profits goes to employees' tax-deferred retirement plans.

* *Performance-sharing.* Standards and predetermined criteria form the basis of this plan, which necessitates creating a fund for incentive awards.

* *Stock-based.* Employees with this plan are provided with the means to acquire employer stock and are encouraged to invest in the organization, which gives them a financial stake in the organization's future success. Employees can purchase or earn these plans through payroll deductions, or they may be structured as a form of employee stock-ownership plans (ESOPs) as defined by the Employment Retired Income Security Act (ERISA). There are two types of stock-based plan:

  - *Nonleveraged ESOP.* The employer contributes stock or cash or provides employees with discounts to buy stock. This type of plan is designed to provide ownership/stake at relatively low cost.

  - *Leveraged ESOP.* The employer borrows from a financial institution or the plan sponsor to finance the organization's stocks rather than contribute the cash or stock directly. This type of plan is sometimes used in seeking wage concessions or other concessions, but it isn't as popular as a nonleveraged plan, because it does not meet the line-of-sight criterion.

EMPLOYEE RETIREMENT INCOME SECURITY ACT

The Employment Retirement Income Security Act (ERISA) established uniform minimum standards to ensure that employee benefit plans are established and maintained in a fair and financially sound manner. They were designed to protect participants and their beneficiaries from private retirement programs. Employers are not required to offer benefits, but if they do, they must conform to ERISA requirements in order to receive tax advantages.

ERISA applies to the private sector and pre-empts any state laws that would, in any way, attempt to regulate employee benefits. It also allows for DOL jurisdiction of reporting, disclosure, and fiduciary responsibility, and IRS jurisdiction over tax-related matters. The Pension Benefit Guaranty Corporation (PBGC) ensures payments of certain pension plan benefits in the event that a private-sector defined-benefit pension plan lacks sufficient funds to pay the promised benefits. Covered plans are required to pay premiums to the PBGC. The law does not cover 401(k) plans or plans that do not have a defined contribution.

ERISA RULES INCLUDE THE FOLLOWING:

* ERISA plans must be operated for the exclusive benefit of the participants or beneficiaries. The employer sponsor must follow the prudent person rule, which prevents employers from taking more risks than a reasonably knowledgeable prudent investor.

* Breaches of the rules that impair the value of plan assets in an individual account must be addressed with the recovery of losses and individuals must be able to

sue a plan sponsor.

* Eligibility requirements for retirement plan benefits must be established.

* Minimum vesting requirements must be established (usually over time). These include
  - *Cliff vesting.* Benefits become 100 percent nonforfeitable after a certain number of years.
  - *Graded vesting.* Benefits become incrementally nonforfeitable over a set period of years.

RETIREMENT ACCOUNTS

The Pension Protection Act (PPA) affects defined benefit plans, defined contribution plans, individual retirement accounts, and other aspects of retirement planning and addresses the following:

* deferral and catch up contributions

* full vestment of defined benefit pension plans over a period of seven years

* the option for employees to automatically enroll in a 401(k) with default contribution levels

* distribution of benefit statements to participants and beneficiaries

* money inherited by beneficiaries

* establishment of requirements for 403(b) plans in nonprofit organizations and making 4039(b) plans more like 401(k) plans

DEFINED BENEFIT PLANS

The retirement benefit amount is based on a formula in the defined benefit plan. The employer must fund the plan to the level required by the formula and assume the responsibility for ensuring that sufficient funds will be available in the plan when required for retirement contributions. Plans are insured by the PBGC, and participating organizations may pay annual per-participant premiums.

DEFINED CONTRIBUTION PLAN

Employees and/or employers pay a specific amount for each participant in a defined contribution plan. Employer contributions are often based upon a percentage of salary or percentage of profits. Once the employer's obligation has been met (contribution), the relationship is fiduciary and administrative in nature. The amount is determined by the level of participation and the fund's performance over the years and is not guaranteed. Types of defined contribution plan include the following:

* *Profit-sharing.* A portion of an organization's profits is distributed to its employees (profits are not required for contributions).
* *Employee stock ownership plan (ESOP).* Stock shares are provided to the employee's account.
* *401(k).* Employees are allowed to take tax-favored pay deferrals toward retirement savings through a payroll deduction.
* *403(b).* Employees of certain tax-exempt organizations are allowed to contribute pretax dollars toward retirement savings.

NONQUALIFIED DEFERRED COMPENSATION PLAN

One way to provide additional benefits to executives is through a nonqualified deferred compensation plan. While this type of plan does not qualify for favorable treatment under ERISA, it allows participants to defer receipt of income (while paying taxes on income), or provide supplemental retirement beyond the limits of the plan. However, the benefits are unsecured and not protected by ERISA and are subject to claims from creditors. They cannot be made employer-wide, and contributions are not deductible. They include the following variations of the plan:

* *Top hat*. Retirement benefits are targeted to a select management group or highly paid employees.

* *457(f)*. This plan applies to tax-exempt nonprofits, which contribute to the funds. The money is paid to the employee at the time of retirement. The plan is a retention strategy because as long as the money is owed by the employer, it is not taxable.

* *Rabbi trust*. Under this plan, a grantor trust is designed to segregate nonqualified deferred compensation benefits from an employer's general accounts.

HEALTH MAINTENANCE

VARIOUS HEALTH-CARE PLANS INCLUDE THE FOLLOWING:

Fee-for-Service. This is a full choice plan and covered employees can go to any qualified physician or hospital and submit claims to the insurance company. The fee is generated when the employee uses health services. These plans are designed to motivate physicians to provide more services. They are used less frequently due to cost and design.

Managed Care. This type of plan seeks to ensure that the treatments a patient receives are medically necessary and provided in a cost-effective manner. There are a variety of organizations offering managed care plans:

- *Health maintenance organizations (HMOs).* These are prepaid "captured health-care plans" that are structured to emphasize preventative care and cost containment. The physician is paid on a per capita/per head basis rather than for the actual treatment provided. Members voluntarily enroll by paying a set monthly or annual fee. They must use HMO physicians and facilities in order to take advantage of low copayments or fees, and there is no need to submit any claims.

- *Preferred Provider Organizations (PPOs).* Insurance companies form PPOs, which are networks of health-care providers who are paid negotiated fees by the insurance company. In return, the health-care providers guarantee a certain number of patients. Services delivered out of the network are charged at a higher rate.

ACTS TO KNOW

RETIREMENT EQUITY ACT

Certain legal protections are provided for spousal beneficiaries of qualified retirees under the Retirement Equity Act (REA). Married participants in plans that provide annuity as the normal form of benefit cannot change their retirement plan benefit distribution elections or spousal beneficiary designations or make an in-service withdrawal without written spousal consent.

PATIENT PROTECTION AND AFFORDABLE CARE ACT

Passed in March of 2010 as a form of health care reform, the Patient Protection and Affordable Care Act (PPAC) applies to all health plans that offer coverage for children up to age twenty-six (and other qualified beneficiaries) and to all plan years beginning on or after September 23, 2010. Employers must opt to go with more generous coverage if state law specifies otherwise.

HEALTH INSURANCE PORTABILITY AND ACCOUNTABILITY ACT

The purpose of the Health Insurance Portability and Accountability Act (HIPPA) of 1996 is to ensure that individuals who leave (or lose) their job can obtain health coverage even if they or a member of their immediate family has a serious illness or injury or is pregnant. A few of the protections it provides include

- limiting exclusions for preexisting conditions to twelve months
- guaranteeing renewability of health coverage as long as premiums are paid
- prohibiting an employer from discriminating and charging higher premiums or denying coverage for poor health or genetics

FAMILY MEDICAL LEAVE ACT

The Family Medical Leave Act (FMLA) allows employees to take up to twelve weeks of unpaid, job-protected leave. It covers employers with fifty or more employees for twenty or more workweeks in the current or preceding calendar year. The act's provisions include the following:

- To be eligible, an employee must have worked a total of twelve months for the employer, for at least 1,250 hours in the twelve-month period, and at a site in which fifty or more employees work within a seventy-five-mile radius.

* The act allows an employee to take up to twelve weeks of unpaid leave in a twelve-month period.

* The twelve-month period can be a calendar year or a fixed year (e.g., fiscal year) from the date the employee's leave begins, or a twelve-month period that rolls back from the date an employee uses an FMLA benefit.

* For married employees, if both spouses work for the same employer, they are limited to a total of twelve weeks of unpaid leave between them to care for a newborn child, or newly adopted, child, or parent.

* Spouses working for the same employer may split their total of twelve weeks. For example, if one spouse takes six weeks of leave to care for a sick parent, the one spouse could take six weeks for a different purpose, such as to care for a sick child.

* If two people living together are not married, they can each take twelve weeks of unpaid leave.

* Employers are required to reinstate employees who take unpaid leave in the same or equivalent position.

* *In loco parentis* refers to job protection for employees who stand in place of a parent with day-to-day responsibilities to care for and financially support a child and employees who care for those who acted as their parents when they were children (e.g., employees who care for their foster parents).

* In 1993, job-protection coverage was added for a serious health condition that requires inpatient hospitalization, or hospice care, residential care, or continuing treatment with a health-care provider. Job-protection coverage added in 2009

addresses employee incapacity with a serious illness for more than three consecutive calendar days, plus two visits to a health-care provider, or one visit to a health-care provider plus a regimen of continuing treatment. The first health-care visit must be within seven days of the incapacity; two or more visits must apply within the first thirty days. For chronic health conditions, the employee must visit a health-care provider at least twice a year.

* Employees have an obligation to make a "reasonable effort" to schedule intermittent leave so as not to unduly disrupt the employer's operations. Intermittent leave occurs when employees take leave as needed.

MEDICAL CERTIFICATION

The FMLA allows HR to make contact with the medical provider but bans a direct supervisor from doing so. If the paperwork is incomplete or insufficient, the employer must designate in writing what information is missing and give the employee seven days to provide it. Employers may request a new medical certification each year for conditions that last longer than a year.

SARBANES-OXLEY ACT

The Sarbanes-Oxley Act of 2002 is a federal law that established sweeping auditing and financial regulations for public companies. Lawmakers created the legislation to help protect shareholders, employees, and the public from accounting errors and fraudulent financial practices. The law was enacted in response to the Enron scandal and other corporate accounting scandals. The law affects defined contribution plans and covers the following:

* *Blackout period.* When an employee is prohibited from directing or diversifying

assets in an account for a certain period of time, the period is called a blackout. The law requires administrators of 401(k) plans and other defined-contribution plans to provide notice to affected participants and beneficiaries at least thirty days in advance of a blackout period.

* *Blackout notice.* Notification must be in writing, and it should clearly communicate the reason for the blackout and identify investments that are affected. Individuals should be advised to evaluate the appropriateness of their current investment decisions in light of the blackout.

* *Whistleblower protection.* The act protects employees who report conduct they reasonably believe violates federal securities laws, SEC rules, or any federal law and includes criminal penalties for any individual who retaliates against whistleblowers.

Did you know that employers are only required to offer three benefits to employees? Those benefits are Social Security, unemployment insurance, and workers compensation.

SOCIAL SECURITY ACT

This program was designed to provide retirement income to older workers, thus freeing up jobs for younger workers and lowering the level of unemployment. Today it provides a basic foundation for American workers and families: retirement, disability, death, and survivor benefits. To qualify for Social Security, workers must work long enough to accrue a specified number of quarters of coverage, generally forty, which takes at least ten years.

UNEMPLOYMENT INSURANCE:

Employers fund unemployment insurance. This was designed during the Great Depression era as a mandatory employee benefit for employees who lost their job through no fault of their own to mitigate the depths of depression and serious impact of any recessionary period. It is administered by individual states, and laws vary by state. Generally, payment is continued for twenty-six weeks.

To be eligible for unemployment, employees must

* be available and actively seeking work, which includes not turning down suitable employment
* not have left the job voluntarily
* not be unemployed because of a labor dispute
* not have been terminated for misconduct
* have worked a minimum number of weeks

WORKERS COMPENSATION

State insurance paid program paid for by the employer, designed to protect workers in case of a work-related injury or disease. This can include permanent and temporary total disability, permanent and temporary partial disability, survivors' benefits, medical expenses, and rehabilitation. Employers assume all costs regardless of who is to blame for the accident. The overall effect has been to reduce the number of court cases, improve safety on the job, and provide prompt treatment and rehabilitation when injuries occur.

MOTIVATION AND PAY

It's important to understand that all employees are not motivated by the same things. The following are the more popular motivational theories that influence reward and recognition theory. Each element of compensation should seek to fulfill a need, physiological or psychological, and achieve a departmental and organizational goal for ROI. The following are theories of motivation.

Maslow's hierarchy of needs. Maslow believed that lower level needs must be relatively satisfied in order for higher-level needs to emerge or serve to motivate behavior. No need is ever fully satisfied, so lower level needs will always have some influence over behavior. Most important is recognition and identification of individual needs for the purpose of motivating behavior.

Herzberg's two-factor theory (content related). This theory finds an employee's job satisfaction is influenced by two separate things: hygiene factors (dissatisfiers) and motivator factors (satisfiers). Hygiene factors are items related to job context. These could be things such as salary, supervision, and company policies. Motivator factors are related to job content and may include items such as responsibility, recognition, and achievement. Employees may like the work itself but are dissatisfied with company policies. Trying to remedy dissatisfaction will not automatically create satisfaction, because these emotions may not have anything to do with what motivates the employee.

Adam's equity theory (process related). This theory is built on the belief that employees evaluate their job inputs in relation to the outputs they receive. They may also compare what they receive to what others receive.

Vroom's expectancy theory (process related). This theory is all about expectation. It is assumed that motivation is determined by the outcomes people expect to occur as as result of their actions. This theory may better explain why people behave the way they do. If employees show up early and stay late, is it because they expect to receive a promotion or raise? The expectancy theory tells us that employees are motivated to behave a certain way because of what they expect the results to be.

TOTAL REWARDS CASE STUDY

(Answers to this case study can be found in the back of this book)

You've been doing a lot for Wine Now, from identifying strategy to outlining training needed for its employees. To your surprise, the work doesn't stop here. We need to spend some time focusing on total rewards.

Many employees may assume that their compensation package is made up of simply money. However, we've recently discovered that it includes much more. Many employers offer a combination of (1)_____ compensation which includes things such as wages, benefits, and bonuses and (2)_____ compensation which may include things such as interesting duties and opportunities for advancement. We can connect total rewards to a number of other elements of HR management. We connect it to staffing by the way we hire. We connect it to talent management as a tool to drive performance and productivity. We connect it to training as an incentive to obtain additional skills and we also see it in the employee/employer relationship.

As you are preparing to develop the compensation strategy for Wine Now, there are some things you should take into account. The basis of many strategies is similar in that organizations want to not only attract top talent but also retain them. We can help facilitate this strategy by ensuring that Wine Now has some of the basic principles for its compensation philosophy. Use the box below to name a few

(3)	Employees like to feel that their monthly income is secure and predictable.	This asks whether employees feel that they can expect their income when it's due.
(4)	The organization must administer the compensation system efficiently and have the financial resources to support it on a continuing basis.	This asks whether the employer can sustain paying the compensation package consistently.
(5)	Compensation must be large enough to attract qualified employees to join the organization and stay.	This asks whether the organization is compensating in line with the market to attract and retain top talent.
Legal	Compensation must be consistent with numerous federal, state, and local laws.	This asks whether the organization is in compliance with federal and local laws.

There are many things that may affect the way a company administers its compensation plan. Some are within its control and others may be beyond its control. We refer to these factors as (6)_____ _____ _____.
With (7)_____ _____, the focus is on things such as the going rate, labor market trends, and cost of living. (8)_____ factors focus on things such as affordability and the overall business strategy.

(9)_____ factors focus on the skills and effort required to do the job. (10)_____ factors focus on the specific performance and experience of a job candidate. These are all factors that must be considered in totality when planning compensation philosophy.

These are a lot of factors to consider when developing the compensation plan. You are probably wondering where you should even begin. A good starting point for establishing pay levels is (11)_____ _____. These data points collect information about the compensation and benefits of other employees in similar industries or in the same geographical region.

So, you've collected the data points of employee compensation in similar organizations. Now it's time to determine the worth of these roles relative to those in your organization. This is what we call a (12) _____ _____. Its basic purpose is to determine the relative worth of a job in order to establish a meaningful pay structure. It's important to understand that this is not the same as a job analysis. The job analysis tells us what employees do at work. As you are working through your plan to evaluate jobs, you may consider one or a combination of the methods methods below:

(13)	This method is a quantitative technique that breaks down the job into compensable factors and assigns points to those factors.	
(14)	This method consists of identifying grades beforehand and writing broad descriptions. After evaluating, the analyst puts them in the class that best matches the description.	

(15)	This method ranks jobs from highest to lowest.	
(16)	This method uses a combination of the point-factor method and the ranking method. It begins with identifying key jobs and job factors and ranking them.	

This has been a lot to consider. You now understand what makes up total compensation, factors that impact how employees are paid, and how you can begin to set the pay structure but there's still more to know.

You know that as Wine Now continues to expand, you will need to hire more employees. At the top of that list is a director of sales. After reviewing the salary surveys, you realize that the pay range for sales directors in your industry is somewhere between $100K and $175K annually, and you need to get a requisition open as soon as possible. Here are the job details:

Position: director of sales

Location: open

Employee type: full time

Incentives: eligible

Bonus: eligible

ESOP: eligible

Midpoint: $125K

Maximum: $150K

Two weeks in, interviews are well under way, and you believe you may have found two solid candidates. Let's take a look at their profiles.

Jackie has over ten years of experience. She's worked for two of the top five companies in the industry. She has a proven track record and is requesting a base salary of $140K. Before we extend an offer, we need to consider the other candidate's profile, but we'd also need to calculate the (17)_____ _____ for both candidates. This helps us to understand the competitiveness of an employee's pay level.

(18) Use the space below to calculate the competitiveness of Jackie's ask.

Amber has over twenty years of experience. She, too, has worked for two of the top five companies in the industry. As Jackie does, Amber has a proven track record and is requesting a salary of $130K with a $30K sign-on bonus, 100 shares vested after one year of employment, and a guaranteed 10 percent profit-sharing incentive after one year of employment.

(19) Use the space below to calculate the compa-ratio of Amber's ask.

If either Jackie or Amber were to request an annual salary of $155K, we would consider them (20)_____ _____. There is still more to consider before you decide between Jackie and Amber. While you are still deliberating on who will be the best candidate for this role, you've also remembered that you still need to hire some additional people for this team. The director will need an administrative assistant along with some others to help build out this team. You've decided to bring Denise over from the Marketing Department. She's been with Wine

Now for some time now and is looking to get experience in a different department.

Fast-forward a month into the role, Denise has come to talk about her hours. We know that Denise is an hourly employee, and we must ensure we are in compliance with (21) _____ _____ _____ _____ when it comes to the number of hours she's working per week, and how we are compensating her. When Denise took the role to support the sales team, her pay was increased to $20 per hour. She wants you to help her understand how much she can expect to see on her paycheck after she worked a total of fifty hours the previous week. Use the space below to calculate the pay for the straight time and what she should be paid for the overtime.

(22) Straight Time Pay: _____

(23) Overtime Pay: _____

(24) Total Pay: _____

You've decided that Amber is the right choice for director of sales. While considering the offer, she wants to understand what benefits the Wine Now is required to offer its employees, and what the organization is doing in excess of that. You know that the total rewards team is still working on building a comprehensive package, but you can definitely provide her with the required benefits. Use the space below to identify those three:

(25) _____

(26) _____

(27) _____

UNIT 5: EMPLOYEE ENGAGEMENT AND LABOR RELATIONS

EMPLOYEE RELATIONS

Employee and labor relations entails the working relationship between employers and employees. It touches several parts of the employee lifecycle and plays a significant role in the following:

* communicating employee and employer rights
* managing grievances
* advocating for progressive discipline processes
* coaching and counseling employees
* enhancing company culture and climate

EMPLOYEE ENGAGEMENT

Many companies spend time measuring employee engagement. Engagement refers to the level of employees' commitment to their jobs. It also measures their willingness to stay with the organization. The three levels of employee engagement are outlined below:

* Engaged. These employees bring their heads and hearts to work. They are highly participative in day-to-day operations and willingly contribute to the company's overarching goals.

- *Disengaged.* These employ0.1875 inr their jobs and the organization to other employees.

Leaders, along with their HR support, can gauge employee engagement and satisfaction through surveys, focus groups, and exit interviews.

EMPLOYEE INVOLVEMENT

Another way to engage employees is through employee involvement strategies, which help employees feel they are owners of the organization. A sense of ownership aids in helping to move the organization forward. Some forms of employee involvement strategies are:

- *Suggestion boxes.* The old-fashioned suggestion box that is rarely opened, let alone utilized, and will not do much for company morale. However, a suggestion box with a kick will involve employees throughout the company.
- *Peer interviewing.* Regardless of a resume, references, or other factors, employees ultimately have to work with new hires. An employee involvement program that allows employees to interview and choose new coworkers can help smooth out the team.
- *Job enlargement.* This is a job redesign strategy implemented to broaden the scope of an individual's role.
- *Job rotation.* This job redesign strategy provides employees with exposure to, and breadth of, new experiences.
- *Job enrichment.* This is a job redesign strategy implemented to provide more authority, accountability, significance, and feedback to an employee's role.

THE UNIONS

Before unions had the right to exist, their existence was uncertain and threatened. Labor leaders had lobbied for the passage of several state and federal laws only to see them nullified or used against unions after they were passed. During the 1800s, four major tactics were used to keep unions from forming:

Conspiracy doctrine. It was assumed that employees who joined together to try and form unions were conspiring against their employer. The most significant definition is that something one person may be allowed to do alone becomes illegal when done by a group.

Court injunctions. Employers would solicit the help of the court to issue an order that would direct a person or group to refrain from pursuing a course of action.

Yellow dog contracts. These contracts were statements that workers were forced to sign stating that they were not members of a union, promised not to join a union, and would not encourage others to do so.

Antitrust statutes. These include, for example, the Sherman Antitrust Act.

Congress knew something had to be done to neutralize the balance between employers and employees. To achieve this balance, the Federal Injunction Act, also known as the Norris LaGuardia Act, was passed to limit the power courts had to intervene in labor disputes, and it also outlawed the enforcement of yellow-dog contracts.

While the Norris LaGuardia Act restricted court interference, it didn't limit the interference of others. Although the act was passed to encourage bargaining, it did not give workers the protection they needed to engage in these activities.

Employers used detectives to spy on union leaders and also to try to stir up trouble by advocating violence and destruction. Many of these union leaders were attacked or killed by people who discouraged union activity. Some employers even hired strike breakers. Their role was to inflict harm on strikers and scare employees from wanting to join a union.

As employers tried to be more subtle, a less violent method of controlling union activity came about in the form of company unions. They appeared to be in the interest of the worker but ultimately never resolved worker issues as they bargained in the interest of the company.

This violence and consistent turmoil signaled to Congress that once again, the playing field for unions and employers needed to be leveled. Because of this, they passed the National Labor Relations Act of 1935, or the Wagner Act. Its primary purpose was to establish the legal rights of workers.

It was designed to be an economic stabilizer and give employees the right to self-organize. And to guarantee those rights, Congress also identified five unfair labor practices (ULPs) and declared them unlawful:

- interference with employees exercising their rights
- employers' domination of, or interference with, the formation of the union
- union members' attempts to influence hiring/employment decisions
- discrimination against, or discharge of, an employee who has filed a charge with the NLRB
- refusal to bargain in good faith

Do you recall what happened the last time we passed a law without any protections? The Wagner Act also established the NLRB and gave it the authority to administer the act in a peaceful way. It was established to protect the rights of employees, employers, unions, and the general public. The NLRB was created to act as a quasijudicial agency and given the authority to conduct secret-ballot union representation elections and to investigate and remedy employer ULPs through judicial-type proceedings. The board's rulings are enforceable in the US Court of Appeals. The NLRA provided an incentive and protection to those who wanted to organize.

Employers began to complain that unions had too many rights. So, Congress stepped in again and created the Labor Management Relations Act of 1947, or Taft Hartley Act. Congress felt that Wagner provided too many powers to unions. This law was passed to neutralize the relationship between employers and unions once again and it focuses on four fundamental concerns:

* ULPs
* rights of employees as individuals
* rights of employers
* national emergency strikes

And just to be sure they hadn't missed anything, the Labor Management Reporting and Disclosure Act, or the Landrum Griffith Act. was passed in 1959 to regulate the internal controls within a union. It is seen as a bill of rights.

THE UNION ORGANIZING PROCESS

When employees become disenchanted with management or when unions target specific employers for unionization, the organization process may begin. The primary goal is to gain official recognition from the employer. Recognition means that the employer recognizes the union as being entitled to conduct collective bargaining on behalf of the workers in a particular bargaining unit, and management has a duty to bargain in good faith. The various steps in the union organizing process are:

1. *Authorization cards.* These cards, or petitions, are signed by employees to indicate they want union representation. At least 30 percent of eligible employees in a union must sign before the NLRB will order an election (known as the 30% rule). Unions prefer to have 50 percent of eligible employees to increase their chance of a successful vote.

2. *Petition for certification.* The petition usually leads to an election supervised by the NLRA. The petition must state if the employer has declined a request for voluntary recognition of the union. The NLRB then decides on one of the two types of representation election:

    a. *Consent.* This is preferred by the NLRB and involves consent by employer and union to waive the pre-election hearing. Both parties agree to issues such as NLRB jurisdiction, bargaining unit composition, balloting procedures, and voter eligibility.

    b. *Directed.* This is an election ordered by the NLRB regional director when the parties are unable to consent to an election, and it occurs after a pre-election hearing on the unresolved issues.

3. *Representation hearing.* Some essential items to know about this hearing are as follows:

- The NLRB must hold the hearing within twelve days of the petition.
- The NLRB establishes the number of employees in the petition compared to the bargaining unit the union is seeking to represent.
- The employer must give names and addresses of affected employees in a work unit verifying the validity and number of signatures.
- Objective considerations must be present or absent for believing the union does not support the majority (employer petitions only).
- The NLRB maintains the privacy of those who have signed a petition.
- If the petition satisfies the 30 percent rule, a conference with both parties is held.
- The employer is required to post in visible places the date and time of the election.

THE NLRB WILL BAR A PETITION FOR AN ELECTION FOR THE FOLLOWING REASONS:

- *Contract.* An existing collective bargaining agreement bars a petition anytime except the thirty days prior to the expiration of a collective bargaining unit.
- *Statutory.* If a valid election has been conducted within the previous twelve months in the same unit, a petition for election is barred.
- *Certification year.* A petition for an election is barred if a union was initially certified during the previous twelve months.
- *Voluntary recognition.* A petition is barred if a reasonable amount of time after the union, informally and voluntarily recognized by the employer, has not elapsed.
- *Blocking charge.* A petition is barred if a ULP charge affecting the proposed unit

is pending.

* *Prior petition.* If a prior election petition was withdrawn by the requesting party within the previous six months, a petition for election is barred.

* *Recognition.* When an employer recognizes a union through a card check, a decertification election is precluded for a minimum of six months and up to twelve months. The final NLRB ruling states that the recognition bar gives employees an opportunity to seek a secret-ballot election to reverse a card recognition. This offers employees a forty-five-day window to petition the NLRB for a decertification election or assist another union in filing a rival petition. Thirty percent of employees must sign the petition. This decision is based on the unreliability of authorization cards and free choice.

EXCELSIOR LIST

The list bears the names and addresses of eligible bargaining unit employees to ensure complete communication from both parties prior to an election.

VOTER ELIGIBILITY

TO BE ELIGIBLE TO VOTE, THE FOLLOWING CONDITIONS ARE REQUIRED:

* Employees must be on the payroll during the payroll period immediately preceding the date of the direction of the election and the period immediately preceding the time of the election.

* Employees on leave of absence with no reasonable probability that they will return and employees who have been permanently laid off or discharged cannot vote.

- Striking voters who have been permanently replaced are eligible to vote in any election conducted within twelve months of the commencement of the strike.

ELECTION CAMPAIGN

EMPLOYERS' AND UNIONS' ADVANTAGES

Employers have a captive audience in their employees and can present their viewpoint to employees during working time. However, employer presentations/speeches must not be within twenty-four hours of the election or make any promises of benefits or threats of reprisals. Union leaders can visit employees at their homes or contact them via telephone or online to discuss the election.

POLLING PLACE

Campaigning by either party in or around the polling place is prohibited. However, literature may be distributed, and oral solicitation may continue outside the prescribed area until voting is over. Union members may continue to campaign as long as they are off company property.

CHALLENGED AND UNCHALLENGED VOTES

Challenges must be made before the individual goes into the booth to vote and challenged ballots are kept separate from unchallenged votes if they have the potential to affect the outcome of the decision. Uncontested votes are tallied immediately after the election.

COUNTING VOTES

If a simple majority (50 percent), *plus one*, cast their vote for union representation, the union is certified. Note that this is not 50 percent of the eligible voters. A tie vote results in no certification. If the union loses, the NLRB could still require the employer to bargain with the association if the employer is found to have committed severe and, or egregious, ULPs.

TAFT-HARLEY ACT

DECERTIFICATION

The Taft-Harley Act provides the means for employees to terminate union representation. This happens when an employee or group of employees circulate a petition containing a written statement that they no longer wish to be represented by their union. Decertification may be filed by an employee, group of employees, or employee representative. The employer may not assist in the preparation or filing of decertification. This process requires signatures by at least 30 percent of employees represented in the bargaining unit covered by the collective bargaining agreement. After a decertification, no elections can be held in the group for one year.

DEAUTHORIZATION

The authority of the bargaining representative may be terminated in a non-right-to-work state. Deauthorization can apply to the representative's authority to negotiate or enforce a union security clause such as union shop or agency shop clause (a requirement that every employee must pay union dues or agency fees).

Deauthorization may be filed at any time (even within twelve months of a certification election), but only one election can be held in any twelve-month period.

PICKETING

An example of the exercise of the right to free speech, picketing usually involves positioning employees at the place of work with signs and banners, and distributing literature to gain media attention and influence the public. The following are forms of picketing:

- *Organizational picketing.* This is done to entice employees to accept the union as their representative.

- *Recognition picketing.* This is done to obtain the employer's recognition of the union as the bargaining representative of the employees and is limited to thirty days.

- *Informational picketing.* This is done to truthfully advise the public that the employer is nonunion and to discourage employees of other employers from delivering goods

- *Primary picketing.* This is aimed at the principal employer and is lawful as long as the strike itself is legal.

- *Common situs picketing.* In this situation, lawful picketing of a primary employer also affects a secondary employer that occupies common premises.

- *Consumer picketing.* This is a form of product boycott by consumers involved such activities as distributing handbills, carrying placards, and urging customers to refuse to purchase products from a particular retailer. It is legal.

- *Secondary picketing.* This is aimed at putting pressure on an organization that is not directly involved in the labor dispute but has a relationship with the employer in dispute (e.g., a manufacturer that provides production components to the employer in dispute). In most cases, neutral employers are protected under the NLRA from subsequent actions. Secondary picketing can be legal when information handbills are distributed that let the public know the union is not picketing the organization that is not in dispute. They must refrain from using banners on the secondary employer's premise. Generally, secondary picketing is not legal. This occurs sometimes when there are multiple retailers on the same property.

UNFAIR LABOR PRACTICES
EMPLOYER ULPS

Employers should not use TIPS when appealing to employees to defeat unionization:

T = threaten

I = interrogate

P = promise

S = spy

TAFT-HARTLEY DEFINITIONS OF ULPS

- carrying out physical violence by obstructing plant entrances, seizing plant equipment, assaulting nonstriking union members or nonunion workers, or destroying property
- threatening economic reprisal (termination or demotion) for nonunion employees
- striking a neutral or third-party employer to force pressure on another company
- engaging, or encouraging employees to engage, in a secondary boycott

* requiring excessive or discriminatory dues

* demanding employer payment for services not performed or not to be performed

* picketing, or threatening to picket, to force an employer to recognize or bargain with another union

* failing to perform duty of fair representation, referring to a union's failure to represent all members fairly and giving members access to solve disputes in court; based on the theory that a union's breach of fair representation renders the grievance and arbitration process useless (e.g., failing to tell an employee that the union has accepted a different remedy than the one the employee sought in arbitration).

* threatening an employer with a strike, in a nonunion shop, if the employer does not terminate an employee who has provoked the union.

* drawing up a union contract requiring the employer to hire only members of the union or employees "satisfactory" to the union

* terminating the existing contract or striking a new one without notifying the employer and conducting mediation

BARGAINING STRUCTURES

There are four types of bargaining structure when it comes to unions. Historically, most labor agreements have been negotiated between a single union and a single employer. However, the growing complexities of bargaining have led to some alternative structures:

Single union single employer bargaining. This is typically one on one. Employers usually negotiate with a single union since it gives them the freedom or the most significant power to position and decide what's acceptable.

Multiemployer bargaining. This is also called pattern bargaining or coalition bargaining. It consists of more than one employer negotiating with a single union. This often happens in construction, retail, or service industries.

Coordinated bargaining. It consists of several unions bargaining with a single employee and increases the power of many small unions dealing with a large employer.

National and local bargaining. This structure consists of the agreement that is negotiated at the national level for economic issues and at the local level for working conditions of other specific problems.

COLLECTIVE BARGAINING

The process by which management and union representatives negotiate the employment conditions for a particular bargaining unit for a designated period of time is called collective bargaining. It covers wages, benefits, and working conditions.

COLLECTIVE BARGAINING AGREEMENT

The day-to-day relationship between the employer and employees in the bargaining unit is governed by a collective bargaining agreement for a specific length of time. Neither party can discontinue negotiations without first attempting in good faith to negotiate a contract. A collective bargaining agreement considers economic conditions, legal and regulatory factors, bargaining precedents, and public and employee opinion.

NLRA COLLECTIVE BARGAINING TOPICS

The three categories of bargaining topics outlined by the NLRA are mandatory, voluntary, and illegal.

- *Mandatory.* These topics include overtime, discharge, discipline, layoff, recall, seniority, promotion, transfer, safety, vacation, holiday, leave of absence, sick leave, some forms of union security, grievance, demotion, assignment, and contractual work, among others.

- *Permissive or voluntary.* Topics include benefits for retired members, settlements of ULPs, and neutrality agreements, among others. Either side can refuse to bargain based on these topics.

- *Illegal.* These topics include closed shops, or discriminatory hiring, among others.

APPROACHES TO CONTRACT NEGOTIATION:

If you work in a union environment or with some form of workers' council, your job may heavily rely on contract negotiations. Many employers are very specific about the need for negotiation skills as they are critical to the employer/employee relationship. Several different approaches can be taken to negotiate agreements between unions and employers or employees and employers. Let's take a closer look at some negotiation strategies.

Positional negotiation. People lock themselves into positions that they find difficult to exit. Parties lose sight of the underlying problems to be resolved, and the emphasis is placed on winning a position.

Principled negotiation. This type of negotiation is based on four premises:

People must be separated from the problem.

The focus must be on interests, not positions.

Options for mutual gain must be created.

Objective criteria must be used.

Distributive bargaining. The outcome of the conflict resolution represents a gain for one party and a loss for the other. Distributive bargaining focuses on taking and defending a position and is usually regarded as the dominant activity in the union-management relationship.

Integrative bargaining. When more than one issue must be resolved, tradeoffs are made, and creative solutions to conflicts are sought to reconcile each party's interests and bring mutual benefits.

Interest-based bargaining. This type of bargaining is also known as mutual gains or win-win bargaining. Parties in conflict look for common ground and attempt to satisfy mutual interests through the bargaining process. The overall goal is consensus decision making.

STRIKES

Employees' refusal to work can involve a concerted slowdown or other concerted interruption of operations. A strike may be used to force concessions or to protest an ULP. Employees' right to strike is protected under the NLRA.

LEGAL STRIKES

* *Sympathy.* The union strikes an employer in support of another union engaged in a dispute with this employer, even though the first union has no conflict with the employer. Organizations seek to restrict sympathy strikes and need to add a specific no-strike clause in the collective bargaining agreement to address this type of strike.

* *Lockout.* Management shuts down operations to prevent employees from working. It is done to avert potential sabotage to facilities, prevent injury to employees who continue to work, and force the union to modify its bargaining strategy.

* *Economic.* During the collective bargaining period, parties fail to reach agreement over terms and conditions of employment, including key economic issues. If the employer hired temporary workers to replace strikers, the temporary workers must be replaced with the remaining strikers, but strikers can only come back if a substantially equivalent position is open, or they can be placed on a preferential hiring list. Usually, even when replacement workers are permanent, most settlements require the return of strikers and the discharge of the replacement workers..

* *ULP.* In the context of a strike, if the employer refuses to bargain, the employer may only hire temporary replacements.

ILLEGAL STRIKES

* *Wildcat.* Work stoppages involving the primary employer-employee relationship that are neither sanctioned nor stimulated by the union are known as wildcat strikes. They violate a no-strike clause in the union-employer bargaining

agreement. This type of strike may take the form of excessive absenteeism for several days, or a work slowdown. Wildcat strikers are not protected under the NLRA and can be terminated or disciplined.

* *Jurisdictional.* Friction between two or more unions working for the same employer results in members of one union stopping work to pressure the employer to assign work to them rather than to the members of the other union. This type of strike occurs mostly in the construction industry. The NLRB is empowered to step in and resolve the issue.

* *Sit-down strikes.* Strikers remain on their employer's premise and take possession of the property, excluding others from entry and making it impossible to hire replacement workers.

UNPROTECTED STRIKE ACTIVITIES

* *Work to rule.* Employees perform only tasks in their job description and refuse to help elsewhere. This type of strike is not unlawful but is not protected.

* *Picket line misconduct and strike violence.* The NLRA does not protect picket line misconduct and violence, and an employer may refuse to reinstate or reemploy employees who are guilty of this conduct.

To combat strikes, employers may try to manage employees' expectations the year before negotiations by providing more information on performance and pay compared with industry standards. Strikes are less likely when employees feel vulnerable because they can be replaced due to outsourcing or the nature of their work.

SAFEGUARDS AGAINST UNIONIZATION

HR CAN TAKE THE FOLLOWING STEPS TO MAINTAIN A UNION-FREE ORGANIZATION:

* The organization's position regarding unionization must be clearly articulated. This includes stating, in the employee handbook, reasons for wanting to stay union-free, and information about organizing cards and how certification elections work.

* Employees must be treated fairly and consistently.

* Access to career opportunities must be available. Many union-free organizations also use job bidding or job posting, which allows the employer to pick from a pool of candidates generated from the job-bidding process instead of publicly posting an opening.

* Promotion decisions must be balanced. Generally, a mixed system blending seniority and ability is preferable to a nonmixed system. In a unionized organization, seniority is given substantial weight.

* There are formal complaint procedures and tools a union can use to provide feedback. Nonunion workplaces should also provide feedback mechanisms and make sure management supports them. Examples of such mechanisms include:
  - *Attitude/climate surveys.*-These a pulse surveys are designed to check the pulse of your organization.
  - *HR/labor relations reviews.* These audit your complaint process
  - *Skip-level interviews.* These are meetings with a higher-level managers.
  - Open-door meetings. These promote transparency and help employees feel more comfortable voicing their concerns

OTHER USEFUL TERMS TO KNOW IN RELATION TO UNIONS INCLUDE THE FOLLOWING:

- *Hot cargo.* This clause in a union contract allows employees to refuse to handle or work on goods shipped from a struck plant, or to provide services to an employer listed on an unfair union list.

- *Open shop.* Employees cannot be forced to join unions or pay dues. Also, they cannot be fired for refusing to do so.

- *Closed shop.* Employees are required to be members of a union as a condition of their employment. Employers may only hire union members.

- *Union shop.* Employees must join the union within a specified amount of time after being hired.

- *Featherbedding.* More workers than needed are hired to do work that is practically pointless (make-work).

- *Agency shop.* Employees are required to pay union dues but *do not* have to join the union officially.

- *Yellow dog contracts.* Employers force new hires to sign yellow dog contracts agreeing to not join a union after being hired.

- *Right to work.* Employees have a right to work whether they are a part of the union or not. In states throughout the USA, NLRA statutes are enforced that prohibit unions from making union membership (payment of union dues) a condition of employment, either before or after hire.

- *Craft unions.* Unions that organize workers of a particular craft/skill are craft unions.

- *Check-off.* Payroll deductions for union dues are called check-offs.

- *Weingarten rights.* Employees in a unionized setting have the right to have a union worker and representative present in investigatory interviews where the employees reasonably believe the investigation may result in disciplinary action.

ALTERNATIVE DISPUTE RESOLUTION

Alternative dispute resolution (ADR) is an umbrella term often used to describe a number of problem-solving and grievance resolution approaches. Generally, it refers to any means of settling disputes outside of the courtroom. It is cost-effective and provides employees and employers with an appropriate and private forum to resolve many workplace disputes. It ultimately reduces the number of cases that end up being litigated in court or informal arbitration.

OTHER FORMS OF ALTERNATIVE DISPUTE RESOLUTION INCLUDE THE FOLLOWING:

- *Ombudsperson.* An employer designates a third party to confidentially investigate employee complaints and mediate disputes. This person may draw an opinion and bring the discussion before the management team. The ombudsperson usually does not settle grievances but may advance unresolved conflicts to other forms of alternative dispute resolution methods.

- *Peer reviews.* A panel of employees are trained to work together to hear and resolve employee complaints. This review panel cannot change policies but may make recommendations.

- *Mediation.* A neutral third party is brought in to help both sides assess the strengths and weaknesses of their arguments. The goal is to negotiate a mutually acceptable, voluntary settlement. The mediator acts more as a facilitator than a judge and cannot impose a solution on either side.

* *Arbitration.* Disputes are submitted to one or more impartial arbitrators, who listen to both sides before making a final determination. The arbitration may be binding or nonbinding. If it is binding, the parties involved must abide by the decision rendered.

NOTE: Some employers make mediation and arbitration a condition of employment, agreed upon in writing.

* *Procedural justice.* This process ensures employees are being treated fairly and with respect.

GRIEVANCE PROCESS

A formal grievance process is essential to increase communication in the organization.

Sometimes, grievances can occur when employees feel dissatisfied with their role or with the organization. They can also happen when the employer/ employee relationship is not clearly defined, when employees feel they are receiving unfair treatment, and when employees feel their management team has violated some part of their employee contractual agreement.

What is important is that during the grievance process, you, as an HR professional, have to make sure your employees feel their complaints will be handled without embarrassment and without tedious procedures that will muddy the employees' grievance claim. Employees must feel their complaints will be evaluated fairly, and they must not be in fear of being fired, mistreated, or retaliated against for submitting and following through with their complaints. It's also important to know that many leaders manage people well but may not have the negotiating skills to effectively come to a resolution with employees filing a grievance complaint. Because of this, many employers are more inclined to use alternative dispute resolution methods, such as arbitration mediation and conciliation, which is a lot more cost-effective than litigation.

Some additional methods of handling grievances include an open-door policy and peer reviews.

EMPLOYEE DISCIPLINE

Employers must provide due process in all situations to avoid legal issues. Failure to provide due process in any termination that does not involve an egregious offense can be used in court. Employees may claim they have been mistreated.

There are three types of punishment: natural consequences, logical consequences, and contrived consequences.

* *Natural consequences.* Behavior can naturally generate undesirable effects. Imagine you tell your child to put on a jacket before leaving home on a cold day, but your child refuses. The natural consequence is that the child becomes cold. This punishment is not imposed by anyone; it just naturally occurs.
* *Logical punishment.* When an employee violates an employer's rule, the employer metes out punishment in alignment with the context of the violated rule. For example, an employer decided to offer an open lunch buffet for free to

all employees. At some point, the employer discovered there was not enough food for everybody because someone was taking extra food home. A logical punishment would be assigning an attendant to serve the food to employees to ensure they're only getting one serving versus multiple servings.

* *Contrived consequences or punishment.* Punishment that's unrelated to the behavior is contrived. Let's imagine you are an employee with a flexible work schedule that allows you to be off every other Friday. You miss an important project deadline one week. Instead of your manager using coaching or some sort of time management training to correct your behavior, your manager decides to take away your flexible work schedule.

PROGRESSIVE DISCIPLINE STEPS

Most issues can be mediated with problem-solving sessions and open dialog. The following four steps are involved:

1. *Initial discussion.* This should be focused on coming up with a solution, not on berating employees, and should be limited to performance issues (not personal). The goal is to resolve the issue before it progresses any further.

2. *Warning.* If a second infraction occurs within a specified amount of time, an official warning letter is issued. Both the problem and the needed correction should be described in specific, objective terms. A signed copy should be kept. The manager should meet with the employee to understand the issue, and the discussion with the employee should be held in private. If possible, the session should end on a positive note.

3. *Second warning.* Another written letter may be provided, and a second private meeting arranged. The employee is reminded again of the possible consequences.

4. *Final written warning.* A deadline for improvement should be provided, and possibly, time off work (suspension). A decision day for accepting the written terms must be specified. The final written warning should clearly state that continuation of the documented issues will lead to termination.

DISCHARGE/TERMINATION OF EMPLOYMENT

Employment at will refers to the employment relationship between employers and employees. It outlines that either is able to terminate employment for any reason so long as it's not discriminatory.

THE EXCEPTIONS TO EMPLOYMENT AT WILL ARE:

- Under the public policy, employees cannot be fired for fulfilling legal obligations or for exercising their constitutional rights (jury duty, filing for worker's compensation, refusing to commit perjury, or whistleblowing).

- An implied contract exists when an agreement is implied from circumstances even though there has been no express agreement between the employer and employee (e.g., the organization's policy of using progressive discipline could mean that an employee cannot be terminated at will).

IN STATES WITH EMPLOYMENT AT WILL, TWO FORMS OF ILLEGAL TERMINATION APPLY:

Retaliatory discharge. An employee is discharged in retaliation for actions that were legal, but contrary to the interests of the employer, such as filing a workers' compensation claim.

Constructive discharge. A court concludes that an employee quits because of intolerable working conditions that the employer created to force the employee to leave.

RISK MANAGEMENT

Risk management should be part of an organization's overall business strategy. Some risk occurs as a natural consequence of regular business operations, such as the risk of injury to construction workers or the potential for false unemployment insurance claims. Other threats come from extraordinary circumstances such as natural disasters or workplace violence. In any case, risks need to be identified so organizations can decide how to deal with them.

Methods for managing risk can be divided into four strategies:

Avoidance. The risk is avoided completely.

Transfer: The risk is transferred to an insurance company or another party.

Mitigation: The impact of the risk is mitigated.

Acceptance: The risk is accepted and the consequences are dealt with.

Occupational Safety and Health Act

The Occupational Safety and Health Act (OSHA) of 1970 states it is the responsibility of each employer to provide a place of employment free from recognized hazards that cause death or serious physical harm to employees. What's vital for you to know about OSHA is that the federal agency enforcing this law is the Occupational Safety and Health Administration. When this act was introduced, it contained a lot of language that employers had difficulty interpreting. Because of this, the agency also introduced the General Duty clause, which states that even if employers don't violate any of the specific standards outlined by OSHA, if they were aware or should have been aware of a hazard that could cause injury or death, they could still be held liable. If employers are still unsure about what to do to be in compliance with OSHA standards, they can request on-site consultations with OSHA officials to help them understand what changes they need to implement or correct.

What's also important to note about OSHA safety standards is that employees have the right to request an OSHA inspection if they believe their working conditions are hazardous. The act protects employees from any sort of retaliation or termination for requesting this type of inspection. They can also refuse to work if they believe they their working conditions pose a significant danger and may cause death or serious physical harm.

One other essential item you may see on your exam paper is OSHA's record-keeping requirements. OSHA's form 301 is used to record an incident. It must be completed within seven calendar days of the incident. OSHA's form 300 is a log of work-related injuries and illnesses that gives employers a compact look at all workplace incidents. It could aid in identifying problems or serve as a means to adjust safety programs. OSHA's form 300A is a summary of work-related injuries and illnesses. Employers must summarize the log at the end of each year.

HAZARD COMMUNICATION STANDARD

Employers are required by the Hazard Communication Standard (HCS) to notify employees when hazardous chemicals are present in the workplace and train employees to work with them safely,

Manufacturers of hazardous chemicals and employers whose employees could be exposed to dangerous chemicals are required to comply with a new label and safety data sheet (SDS) requirements that conform to the United Nations' globally harmonized system of classification and labeling of chemicals (GHS).

The right-to-know standard requires all employers to develop and communicate, in writing, information on the hazards of products used in the workplace. The primary tool engaged in conveying the dangers of a substance is the safety data sheet (SDS).

EMPLOYEE AND LABOR RELATIONS CASE STUDY

(Answers to this case study can be found in the back of this book)

You've been working with Marc Merlot a lot over the past few weeks on building and understanding the strategy he has for Wine Now. He is lucky to have you on his team. Now it's time to get to the heart of what will make Wine Now successful: everything related to Wine Now's people.

The employer and employee relationship can be a tricky one. Since the beginning of time, we've tried to find a way to make this relationship an amicable and agreeable one for both parties. However, it's been a bumpy road. Let's take a look at how we've been able to make some progress through the years and how you will be able to help Marc.

(1) _____ _____ is the working relationship between an employer and an employee that encompasses the rights of each party, how decisions are made, and how problems are resolved. We now have this term that helps to define how the employment relationship should work. That should have been enough right? Far from right.

You have some responsibilities in this space, and you need to help Marc and your managers understand what those responsibilities are. Check all boxes that apply in the table below:

(2)

Establishing and communicating employee and employer rights and responsibilities
Managing grievances in response to decisions made about the employee
Employing positive employee relations strategies to enhance company climate and culture
Coaching and counseling employees where appropriate
Managing the process of union organization and collective bargaining
Disciplining and terminating employees in accordance with legal guidelines to manage risk

Before you can do your job effectively, you first need to provide Marc with some data on the make-up of his organization. You want to understand the degree to which employees are committed to their jobs and the organization, their willingness to remain with the organization and work hard to make it succeed, and their enthusiasm in completing their work and helping their coworkers. This is sometimes referred to as **(3)**_____ _____. As you know, there are levels of engagement. In the chart below, match the employees' level with the letter A, B, or C.

A. Engaged B. Actively Disengaged C. Not Engaged

(4)		Employees putting in their time and going about their work with little energy or passion, but not interfering with others
(5)		Employees working with vigor, dedication, and absorption
(6)		Employees who are unhappy about their work, actively complain about their job and the company, and undermine what their engaged colleagues are trying to achieve

Now you know which buckets these employees belong in, you need to get a better understanding of how you can make them more engaged and satisfied in their roles. There are four theories that have been identified to help explain whether employees will feel satisfied or dissatisfied. They fall under the umbrella of the job (7)_____ _____ theory. You need to help Marc understand that no two employees are alike. In addition to identifying what will help employees feel satisfied, you also need to ensure you are able to measure that satisfaction.

THREE OF THE MORE COMMON METHODS YOU CAN DO THIS ARE THE FOLLOWING:

(8)	This method provides an opportunity to gain candid information on conditions in the organization as well as specific issues that may have contributed to the employee's decision to leave.

(9)	This method can be used to assess employee perceptions about the work environment, and provide formal documentation of important organizational issues.
(10)	This method can provide an in-depth look at specific issues raised during a survey.

You've got a fair amount of information to present to Marc. However, the heavy lifting hasn't even begun. Here's what we know:

* the basics of the employer and employee relationship
* employees who are engaged and not engaged
* job satisfaction and how you can measure it

Now it's time to see how you can possibly improvement the job satisfaction of these employees. Sometimes, a small tweak to a role can make a significant impact. We often refer to this as **(10)**_____ _____.

With the data you've gathered, a few specific scenarios have surfaced. Marc expects you to review each situation and make a recommendation.

Scenario 1: Business for Wine Now has started to pick up. Who knew that people would enjoy wine delivered to their doorstep? As the orders have increased, the need for employees who have the capacity to do more is critical. Matthew works in the client-facing department of Wine Now. As customers place orders, he is responsible for taking the order and collecting the payment. For returning customers who need to update their payment information or address, Matthew has to hand them off to Frederick. If Matthew were able to take the orders, collect the payments, and make the updates to customer accounts, this would be considered **(11)**_____.

Scenario 2: Recently, numerous customers have raised questions about the different types of wine they're ordering, such as information on originating vineyards and palatable pairings. You've recognized that the client ordering process has become twice as long as it needs to be because Matthew has to transfer calls to Roberta on the education team to answer client questions, and then she has to transfer the answers back to Matthew to finish the transaction. Allowing Matthew to work on the education team to learn how to answer client questions and Roberta on the client team to learn transactions would be an example of **(12)**_____.

Scenario 3: Matthew and Roberta are very valuable assets to Wine Now. Both are now cross-trained on multiple facets of the business. Marc is looking to expand the offerings of Wine Now and needs some insight on what his customer base is looking for. Since Matthew and Roberta interact with customers daily, he has decided to create a work group that focuses on the strategy of Wine Now In addition to their current responsibilities, both Matthew and Roberta will be responsible for brainstorming with Marc through products, service offerings, implementation, and customer education on a weekly basis. Marc has complete trust in their abilities and believes that with their help, Wine Now will push the organization forward. These additional duties are often labeled as **(13)**_____.

You assumed providing tweaks to some of the jobs within Wine Now would increase employee engagement. Unfortunately, Matthew and Roberta have been speaking to other employees about how they feel overworked and underpaid. To your surprise, many of the other employees feel the same as Matthew and Roberta and are considering union representation. You recall that none of the employees signed **(14)**_____ _____ _____, which commit them to promise not to join a union or encourage others to do so. You also know that the **(15)** _____ _____, which would have prohibited group activity in lieu of solo activities is now illegal.

You've never managed a union, so not only do you need to get educated but you also need to notify Marc. After learning of the possibilities, Marc wants to know if the courts should be involved. You let him know that the **(16)**_____ _____ Act outlawed court involvement in labor disputes. It's completely unlawful to spy on these employees and form any company unions to try and remedy the employee issues because the **(17)**_____ _____ has guaranteed the right for employees to organize and bargain collectively. It also established the **(18)**____ ____ ____ ____ which performs two major functions: conducting representation elections and resolving ULPs.

Although the aforementioned act provides employees with the right to organize, you feel that it provides too much power to unions and know there has to be something that provides guidelines on what the unions cannot do. Luckily for you, the **(19)**_____ _____ Act came along in 1947 to identify ULPs for unions. And to be sure nothing was missed, you also learned that the **(20)**

Cari Hawthorne

_____ _____ Act was enacted to regulate internal controls of labor unions (think of it like a bill of rights).

Now, while you were off getting educated, Matthew and Roberta have rallied the troops. They've decided that they wanted to move forward with union representation, but there are a few things that must take place. Use the charts below to list the steps.

| **(21)** Step 1 | |

There are 700 employees at Wine Now. How many employees are needed for Matthew and Roberta to proceed to the next step? Complete the calculation **(22)**:

700 X ____% = _____ (total number of cards needed) Do they have enough?

| **(23)** Step 2 | If Marc were to decide to have a directed election, what happens next? |

| **(24)** Step 3 | |

Before you proceed to the next step, Roberta and Matthew must make sure there are no **(25)**_____ _____ and they have asked you to submit an **(26)** _____ to the NLRB. This list includes all eligible employees.

Although Marc is upset by all of this, your role is to inform him that he must not do anything of the following before election: **(27)**

179

Hr Defined Workbook

| T_____ | I_____ | P_____ | S_____ |

Matthew and Roberta are tracking what they need. You've educated Marc. Now it's time for Step 4: The **(28)**_____.

After it has taken place, it's time to count the votes. Of the 700 employees, 500 are eligible to vote, and 50 have decided that they would not vote. Of the remaining eligible employees, 450 voted. How many votes are needed to certify the union? **(29)**_____

Fast-forward to after the election, the union is now certified, but Matthew and Roberta are afraid that they've made the wrong decision. They've been dissatisfied with the union officials and are looking for ways to hold the leadership accountable. They can do this through **(30)**_____. If this method doesn't satisfy their expectations, they can also pursue **(31)**_____ which would allow them to get rid of the union.

After a union has won an election and negotiated an agreement, it may face the problem of member apathy: Many members do not want to continue supporting union activities or paying union dues. Consequently, unions have designed several arrangements to ensure continued membership. These include some of the following:

Term	Definition	Is this Legal?
(32)	Employees cannot be forced to join unions or pay dues, and they cannot be fired for refusing to do so.	
(33)	Employees are required to pay union dues but *do not* have to officially join the union.	

(34)	Employees must join the union after a specified amount of time following hire.	
(35)	Employees are required to be members of a union as a condition of their employment. Employers may only hire union members.	

CASE STUDY ANSWERS

BUSINESS MANAGEMENT CASE STUDY

1. Corporate governance

2. Organizational strategy or business strategy

3. Vision

4. Mission statement

5. Strategy

6. Perfect

7. Imperfect

8. SWOT analysis

9. First three statements

10. Policies

11. Employee handbook

12. Incremental budgeting

13. Formula-based budgeting

14. Zero-based budgeting

15. Cash flow
16. Income
17. Balance
18. Gross profit margin
19. $675K = 72%
20. HR audit
21. Key performance indicators
22. Balanced scorecard
23. Customer perspective
24. Business/internal processes
25. Learning and growth
26. Outsourcing
27. HRIS
28. Differentiation
29. Integration
30. Functional
31. Decentralized
32. Climate
33. Diversity and inclusion
34. Transformational

35. Transactional

36. Corporate social responsibility

37. Expatriate

38. Third country national

39. Local national

40. Ethnocentric

41. Polycentric

TALENT PLANNING AND ACQUISITION CASE STUDY ANSWERS

1. Civil Rights Act

2. Title VII

3. EEOC

4. Fifteen

5. Civil Rights Act of 1991

6. BFOQ

7. Bona fide occupational qualification

8. Intentional

9. Unintentional

10. Four-fifths rule

11. 100/180 = .55% 60/200 = .80% 55/80 = 66% adverse impact exists

12. Take it seriously

13. Respond immediately
14. EEO-1
15. 11246
16. Affirmative action plans
17. Age discrimination and employment
18. Succession planning
19. What talent do we have?
20. What talent do we need?
21. Delphi technique
22. Replacement chart
23. Job analysis

LEARNING AND DEVELOPMENT CASE STUDY ANSWERS

1. Education
2. Training
3. Tacit
4. Explicit
5. New employee orientation
6. Onboarding
7. ADDIE
8. Visual

9. Auditory

10. Kinesthetic

11. Reaction

12. Learning

13. Behavior

14. Results

TOTAL REWARDS CASE STUDY ANSWERS

1. Financial

2. Nonfinancial

3. Provide security

4. Cost-benefit effective

5. Adequate

6. Determinants of pay

7. External factors

8. Internal

9. Job

10. Individual

11. Compensation/salary surveys

12. Job evaluation

13. Point Factor

14. Classification

15. Ranking

16. Factor comparison

17. Compa-Ratio

18. 112%

19. 104%

20. Red circled

21. FLSA

22. 800

23. 300

24. 1100

25. Workers compensation

26. Social Security

27. Unemployment

EMPLOYEE ENGAGEMENT AND LABOR RELATIONS CASE STUDY ANSWERS

1. Employee relations

2. All should be checked

3. Employee engagement

4. Not engaged

5. Engaged

6. Actively disengaged

7. Satisfaction

8. Exit survey

9. Focus Groups

10. Job design or job redesign

11. Job enlargement

12. Job rotation

13. Job enrichment

14. Yellow dog contracts

15. Conspiracy doctrine

16. Norris Laguardia

17. Wagner Act

18. NLRB

19. Taft-Hartley

20. Landrum Griffith Act

21. At least 30% of eligible employees must sign authorization cards.

22. 700 x .30% = 210 (Yes)

23. A petition is filed by an employee.

    a. A representation election is ordered by the NLRB.

24. Verify signatures on cards

    a. Representation hearing

    b. Voter eligibility

    c. Time and place of the election

25. Bars to election

26. Excelsior list

27. Threaten, interrogate, promise, spy

28. Election

29. 226 (recall 50% + 1)

30. Deauthorization

31. Decertification

32. Open shop—legal

33. Agency shop—illegal in right-to-work states

34. Union shop—illegal in right-to-work states

35. Closed shop—illegal

Made in the USA
Monee, IL
05 November 2020